Penguin Education

Penguin Modern Economics Texts
General Editor: B. J. McCormick

Microeconomics
Editor: B. J. McCormick

Analytical Welfare Economics
D. M. Winch

D. M. Winch

Analytical Welfare Economics

Penguin Education

Penguin Education
A Division of Penguin Books Ltd,
Harmondsworth, Middlesex, England
Penguin Books Inc, 7110 Ambassador Road,
Baltimore, Md 21207, USA
Penguin Books Australia Ltd,
Ringwood, Victoria, Australia

First published 1971
Reprinted 1973
Copyright © D. M. Winch, 1971

Made and printed in Great Britain by
Cox & Wyman Ltd, London, Reading and Fakenham
Set in Monotype Times

Penguin Modern Economics Texts

This volume is one in a series of unit texts designed to reduce the price of knowledge for students of economics in universities and colleges of higher education. The units may be used singly or in combination with other units to form attractive and unusual teaching programmes. The volumes will cover the major teaching areas but they will differ from conventional books in their attempt to chart and explore new directions in economic thinking. The traditional divisions of theory and applied, of positive and normative and of micro and macro will tend to be blurred as authors impose new and arresting ideas on the traditional corpus of economics. Some units will fall into conventional patterns of thought but many will transgress established beliefs.

Penguin Modern Economics Texts are published in units in order to achieve certain objectives. First, a large range of short texts at inexpensive prices gives the teacher flexibility in planning his course and recommending texts for it. Secondly, the pace at which important new work is published requires the project to be adaptable. Our plan allows a unit to be revised or a fresh unit to be added with maximum speed and minimal cost to the reader,

The international range of authorship will, it is hoped, bring out the richness and diversity in economic analysis and thinking.

B.J.McC.

Contents

Editorial Foreword

Welfare economics is back in fashion. In the 1950s it had seemed to become a sterile subject, suitable only for those who were perverse enough to enjoy mental gymnastics. The inability of the market to solve all problems has, however, forced economists to re-examine the issue of policy re-introduction. Traffic congestion, poverty, pollution and *poverty* 'growth for what' have raised once more all the difficulties of reconciling various interest.

Economic analysis examines how economic agents, acting as producers and consumers, produce a system which attempts to be both efficient and equitable. Unfortunately, an ideal system seems to be a mirage since there are many ethically acceptable (to someone) systems. Given the difficulties of delineating such a system, the economist is forced to examine the distribution of power in society. He is forced to see his subject as political economy.

Professor Winch has written an original and rigorous book on the subject of how change might be brought about in society. In many chapters he has produced new and interesting verbal and geometric ideas. And he has consciously introduced the ethical and political aspects of desired change, and thereby prevented us from regarding economics as a branch of applied mathematics.

B.J.McC.

Preface

The basic apparatus of analytical welfare economics is a branch of the subject taken for granted at all levels. The student often proceeds to higher degrees without giving it serious study, though the advanced literature in his chosen field will often assume familiarity with it. Welfare economists write critiques of their subject on the assumption that their readers will be familiar with what it is that is being criticized. Practitioners of applied (welfare) economics all too often pay lip service to the role of social values in such way as to emphasize only that they have never really thought about what a social value is. The welfare economist who questions the premises on which the policy implications of their research necessarily depend is popularly dismissed as an unworldly philosopher who has nothing constructive to say about the pressing issues of the real world.

This disregard of, and disrespect for, the very foundation on which rest all branches of economics that have any relevance at all to the real world of economic issues and policies has led me over the past decade to attempt to initiate honours under-graduates and first-year graduate students into the mysteries of the subject. Many students have expressed the need for a textbook that provides a coherent outline, a background against which they can view in better perspective their reading of journal articles and advanced books. When I was invited to write such a book for the Penguin Modern Economics Texts, I welcomed the challenge to produce the missing work myself. The result is, of course, based on my own lectures and seminars, and the coverage essentially that which has emerged over the years from the interplay of what I considered most important and my students considered most interesting. I offer it to a wider audience in the hope that it might provide an outline of a one-term course on which fellow instructors can proceed to improve; that it might provide for serious students who do not have the opportunity to study the subject directly for credit at least a baptism in the muddy waters of collective rationality; that economists who missed the subject in their formal training might find it a relatively painless way to fill a few gaps; and that perhaps some of my old students might at last discover in their leisure what it was I was talking about.

My debt to those who developed the subject is obvious. Less apparent, but equally real, is my gratitude to my teachers, colleagues and students, past and present, with whom discussion and argument has shaped this book as it shaped my thinking. To the universities at which I have studied and taught go my thanks for the environment in which that intercourse flourished.

1 Introduction

The nature of welfare economics

Welfare economics is the study of the well-being of the members of a society as a group, in so far as it is affected by the decisions and actions of its members and agencies concerning economic variables. These variables include the extent and nature of the use of factors of production, the types and quantities of goods and services produced both individually and collectively, and the distribution of the benefits and costs resulting from economic activity among the members of society. Welfare economics differs from the economics of individual consumer behaviour and the behaviour of the firm, being concerned with the extent to which the objectives of the society as a whole are fulfilled rather than the private objectives of its members. The objectives of the society are not clearly distinct from the aims and ambitions of the individuals who comprise it, for if the people as individuals are better off then they are better off as a group. But a study of economics based on individual behaviour leaves unanswered some of the most pressing problems concerning the appropriate policy of the society. The private interest and the public interest can and do conflict. If a particular course of action would result in some persons being privately better off and some worse off, the economics of individual behaviour alone stops short of telling us whether it is on balance a desirable policy. Welfare economics is concerned with such issues and attempts to shed light on the relative merits of different forms of organization of the entire economic system as well as the issues involved in a particular decision to be made by government.

It is not possible for economic analysis to determine what the objectives of society ought to be, nor whether a particular social state is better than another. Such questions are the subject matter of moral and political philosophy. The role of analytical welfare economics is two-fold: to pinpoint the issues about which value judgements as to the objectives of the society must be made; and to reason from those objectives, whatsoever they may be, to conclusions as to the appropriateness of particular policies as means of achieving them.

A policy is a deliberate course of action. Whether or not it is appropriate depends upon both the nature of the objective that is sought and the constraints of the economic system. The constraints are defined by positive economics, which is concerned with the outcome of various economic situations. It reasons from technical and behavioural assumptions that are in principle testable. Assumptions may be made about the properties of production functions, e.g. that they exhibit diminishing returns, and such assumptions can be tested by factual observations. Behavioural assumptions are made about the actions of firms and individuals; that the former attempt to maximize profit and the latter utility. From such premises positive economic analysis reasons that the short-run competitive-supply curve is normally upward sloping, being the relevant portion of the marginal-cost curve, while the demand curve is normally downward sloping. By such chains of reasoning positive economics enables us to predict the consequences of a proposed policy. If, for example, it is proposed that a tax be imposed on luxury goods and the proceeds used to pay family allowances to poor families, positive economics would enable us to predict that if the policy were implemented fewer resources would be devoted to luxury goods and more to those goods for which poor families with children have a high income elasticity of demand. Statistical analysis might indicate which goods these are. At the same time there will be redistributive effects. The users of the luxury goods in question will be worse off and poor families better off. Indispensable though such predictions are, they cannot alone tell us whether the policy is a good one until they are related to the objectives. If it is desired to discourage the consumption of cigars and champagne and to redistribute income from the users of those commodities to poor families, then the policy of taxing cigars and champagne to pay family allowances may be appropriate. But if there was no desire to discourage the consumption of cigars and champagne as such, the objective being purely to redistribute income from rich to poor, then progressive income taxes might have been more appropriate than commodity taxes. Similarly, if the objective was to benefit the children of poor families, then subsidized milk and bread might have been a more appropriate way of paying transfers than family allowances that might largely be spent on cigarettes and beer. This is a simple example, but it illustrates a fundamental truth. One cannot assess the appropriateness of a particular policy, nor choose among alternative policies, unless one pays attention both to the probable consequences of those policies and the objectives that are sought. Analytical welfare economics is concerned with the methodology of such assessments.

If we always had the necessary information in the right form, the assessment of alternate policies would be so simple that the complicated edifice of welfare economics would be unnecessary. If we knew all the relevant supply and demand curves and all markets were perfectly competitive, and we knew exactly from and to whom it was desired to transfer income, and whether the consumption of particular commodities was to be encouraged or discouraged, then the devising of an appropriate policy would be a simple matter. In practice, however, we rarely have the relevant information in a convenient form. Microeconomic analysis has accordingly developed the theories of production, costs, consumer behaviour and markets in an effort to enable us to infer what the relevant forces are and what changes in them can be expected to ensue from given policies. Welfare economics similarly attempts to unravel the objective side of the problem. Whether we want to tax or subsidize people, leaving them free to decide how to spare or spend the money, or alternatively to tax and subsidize commodities, so as to influence the way in which they spend their money, will depend on more fundamental value judgements. If our society is consistent in its objectives then we should be able to infer from our fundamental values what the corresponding specific objectives in a particular case will be. Observation of the policies adopted in specific instances can enable us to infer something about the underlying fundamental values, if we assume policy makers to be rational, just as revealed-preference theory enables us to infer certain properties of individuals' utility functions. If we observe policy decisions in different instances such that they imply conflicting fundamental values, then we know that either there was a change in those fundamental values between the occurrences of the instances in question, or, if this can be ruled out, that the policy maker was inconsistent and the policies might then be offsetting each other at a fundamental level that on superficial examination alone did not appear to be involved.

The logic of rational choice

All economics is concerned with the making of choices. Households choose what kinds and quantities of goods and services to buy with their incomes, and how to earn those incomes by the sale of factor services. Firms choose what kinds and quantities of factors to buy and goods to produce. Governments choose policies. The end product of the whole set of such choices made within an economy, brought about by the interaction of the forces that they generate, is a particular social state. In analysing the choice process and the consequences of choices, economics relies on a standard form of the choice situation. The chooser has a particular objective that he seeks to achieve, but he is constrained by forces beyond his control to a particular range of courses of action from among which he can choose. The economic problem of scarcity manifests itself in the fact that the constraint is binding, that is it does not permit the complete achievement of the objective. The chooser then tries to achieve his objective as fully as possible. If rational, he will maximize the extent to which his objective is achieved.

For the purposes of analysis it is convenient to express the objective as an index which the chooser attempts to maximize (or minimize). If stipulated in functional form such an index can be quite general, but its expression in this form permits us to use the technique of marginal analysis or the differential calculus. By such methods we can derive a rational choice for any given objective and constraint, but we must have both an objective and a constraint, and we must keep clear which is which. Let us briefly review the way in which this method is applied in the analysis of the household and the firm, for we shall then be able to appreciate better the problems inherent in the analysis of choices facing the society as a whole.

In the theory of consumer behaviour the decision maker is an individual or a single household, which is treated analytically as though it were a single individual. The complex psychological problems concerning what motivates the individual, i.e. what determines his objectives, are avoided by the device of a utility function. The consumer is said to maximize utility, and utility is defined as that which the consumer attempts to maximize. This truism is completely general and cannot be false. Since he is motivated to make choices by a desire to achieve his objective we can further say that the level of utility achieved depends upon the choices he makes. If he is choosing among goods, utility is a function of the volumes of goods acquired. The nature of the dependence of utility on goods acquired can be expressed as a function

$$U = U(X_1, \ldots, X_g, A_1, \ldots, A_f),$$

which can be plotted as an indifference map. If the arguments are goods X, i.e. things of which he would rather have more than less, then it is an increasing function (first partial derivatives are positive); if bads A, i.e. things of which he would rather have less than more, it is a decreasing function (first partials are negative). In this way the amounts of various types of work done (factors sold) can be treated as negative goods. The constraint derives from a set of prices which must be paid for goods acquired, or can be received for factors sold, and can be expressed in the form

$$\Sigma P_i X_i - \Sigma P_j A_j = 0,$$

where savings are treated as a good. This is the budget constraint. We can then maximize the utility function, subject to the constraint, by the techniques of calculus, or find the tangency point between an indifference curve and the budget constraint by geometry. If the second-order conditions (curvature of the indifference curves) are appropriate, we have a maximum solution and can derive the appropriate volume of each commodity to buy and factor to sell.

The behaviour of an entrepreneur can be analysed in a completely analogous way, although the conventional model of the competitive firm is normally stated in a different form as the result of a simplifying assumption. If the entrepreneur is assumed to maximize his utility function, like any other individual, we have the objective function

$$U = U(X_1, \ldots, X_g, A_1, \ldots, A_f).$$

The distinguishing feature of the entrepreneur is that he does not sell his services at a contractual price, but combines them with other factors that he buys to produce goods which he sells. His income is the excess of the value of products sold over the value of factors purchased. The return for his services is not a simple wage rate but a residual derived from both the prices he pays and receives for factors purchased and products sold, and the production function.

The comparable models of the household and the entrepreneur may be stated formally as follows:

Let each household consume a subset G of goods X, and provide a subset F of factors A, while each entrepreneur purchases a subset K of factors B and sells a subset H of products Y; let I represent the individual's income, and π the pure profits of the firm.

The choices facing the household can now be represented as;[1]

1. **1** is the general form of the utility function, stating in a particular case the way in which utility depends upon consumption of goods and provision of factor services. **2** is the budget constraint that limits total expenditure on goods (including saving) to income earned. **3** states that income depends on the provision of factor services. **4** is derived from **2** and **3**, while **5** defines **3** as the total value of factor services sold.

maximize $U = U(X_1, \ldots, X_g, A_1, \ldots, A_f)$, **1**

subject to the constraint $\Sigma P_i X_i = I$, **2**

where $I = \phi(A_1, \ldots, A_f)$. **3**

Thus $\Sigma P_i X_i - \phi(A_1 \ldots, A_f) = 0$ **4**

and $\phi(A_1, \ldots, A_f) = \Sigma P_j A_j$. **5**

The relevant prices are yielded by the goods-supply functions and factor-demand functions as these face the household. In the competitive model prices are assumed to be beyond the control of the individual.

The corresponding choices facing the entrepreneur can be represented as;[1]

maximize $U = U(X_1, \ldots, X_g, A_1, \ldots, A_f)$, **1**

subject to the constraint $\Sigma P_i X_i = I$, **2**

where $I = \psi(A_1, \ldots, A_f)$. **3a**

Thus $\Sigma P_i X_i - \psi(A_1, \ldots, A_f) = 0$ **4a**

and $\psi(A_1, \ldots, A_f) = \Sigma P_i Y_i - \Sigma P_j B_j = \Sigma P_j A_j + \pi$. **5a**

The relevant prices are yielded by the product-demand functions and factor-supply functions facing the firm; and the goods-supply functions and factor-demand functions for alternate uses facing the entrepreneur in his capacity as a household. All prices are assumed to be beyond his control in the competitive model.

The relevant quantities A_j, B_j, Y_i are constrained by the production function

$$F(Y_1, \ldots, Y_h, B_1, \ldots, B_k, A_1, \ldots, A_f) = 0. \qquad \textbf{6}$$

Comparison of these statements of the choice situations facing the household and the firm shows that they are identical in terms of the objective **1** and similar in the constraint **4**. The distinction lies in the assumptions concerning the nature of **5**. In the case of the household we assume that factors are sold in quantifiable units at given prices. In the case of labour this

1. **1**, **2**, **3a** and **4a** are analogous with the previous **1**, **2**, **3** and **4**. **5a** defines income as the excess of the value of products sold over the value of factors bought, which is in turn equal to the value of factor services provided by the entrepreneur plus pure profit.

might represent number of hours worked times the wage rate per hour, or number of operations performed times the piece rate per operation. The income of the entrepreneur includes the pure profit term and this results from the nature of a set of decisions made in the operation of the firm, which are constrained by market conditions for factors and products and the production function. The income of the entrepreneur differs from that of other households in that it is dependent not simply on the amount of work done, but on the outcome of decisions made in the choice situations facing the individual *qua* entrepreneur.

In the context of choice analysis, the distinguishing feature of the entrepreneur is that his income depends upon his performance at his job rather than solely upon some defined quantity of work done. Profit is an index of performance. Judged by this characteristic a far greater proportion of the labour force are engaged in the 'entrepreneurial' function than is commonly supposed. In a dynamic context the existence of promotion prospects, where promotion depends upon the quality of decisions made in the performance of salaried employment, would be enough to nullify the simple form of **5**, though nothing as simple as a production function might be substituted therefor.

The simple classification of economic units into households and firms grossly oversimplifies the real world. If classify we must, there are not two types of decision-making unit but three. All households *qua* consumers are subject to the objective **1** and the constraint **4**. They may be classified into three groups: (a) those sellers of defined factors for whom **5** holds; (b) those engaged in the decision-making function in firms for whom **5a** (together with **6**) holds; and (c) the majority for whom no simple form of **5** can be stated. Indeed if we make the normal assumptions implicit in the elementary treatment of the theory of the firm, namely that the entrepreneur knows his production function and the markets for factors and products, then **5a** is completely defined. There is then no essential difference between the choice situations facing the household and the entrepreneur; each tries to maximize a utility function which encompasses both goods consumed and factor services performed; each is constrained by the fact that total expenditure on goods (including saving) must be equal to total income received from factors employed; and each knows the way in which income will be determined by the disposition of factors owned. The concept of the entrepreneur as risk taker is irrelevant in a world of certainty. More complex problems arise with uncertainty, but they arise just as much for households as for firms. The individual worker who is uncertain about the job security and promotion prospects in different occupations, or about the way in which income will respond to the efforts he devotes to his job, faces problems analytically analogous with those of the entrepreneur who is uncertain about how the price of his product (and therefore his income) will respond to the volume of his output.

The implications for welfare economics of this review of the theory of choice are of fundamental importance. The objective of both households and entrepreneurs is to maximize utility. The constraints encompass the rates of return to factors which are endogenously determined. The exogenous constraint is the production function. The scarcity of resources can be encompassed as boundary constraints on individuals' choices. The analogous statement of the choice situation facing the society as a whole is to maximize a social welfare function, dependent positively on individuals' utility levels, subject to a transformation function for the economy. This is the essence of Paretian welfare economics, which we shall examine in some detail in later chapters. Before doing so, however, we shall consider the simplified models of the household and the firm which are commonly used in microeconomics, and show their implications for welfare economics.

The factor side of the household is commonly assumed away to isolate the theory of consumer behaviour. The normal assumption is that the income of the household is fixed, either because the quantities of factors sold are exogenously determined or by assuming that $\partial U/\partial A_i = 0$ up to some maximum volume, so that the maximum income that can be earned becomes the rational amount to earn. The effect is to exclude factors from the relevant variables. The choice situation then becomes;

maximize $\quad U = U(X_1, \ldots, X_g),$ **1b**

subject to $\quad \Sigma P_i X_i - \tilde{I} = 0,$ **4b**

where $\tilde{I}$ is exogenously determined.

The corresponding simplification of the entrepreneur's behaviour involves the assumption that his utility function excludes the variables about which decisions are made in the firm. Either the efforts of the entrepreneur are assumed to be fixed, or he is assumed to be indifferent about how hard he works, i.e. the extent to which he utilizes the factors he owns in the production process. The choice situation then becomes;

maximize $\quad U = U(X_1, \ldots, X_g),$ **1b**

subject to $\quad \Sigma P_i X_i - (\tilde{I}' + \pi) = 0,$ **4c**

where $\tilde{I}'$ is the total implicit costs of the firm (or the normal rate of profit). The role of the entrepreneur *qua* consumer is now the same as that of any other consumer. The pure profit π is not dependent on any variable that enters into the utility function. Maximization of utility therefore requires independent maximization of π, and we have the standard assumption that the firm seeks to maximize profit.

The consequences of the simplifying assumptions for welfare economics have been enormous. Exclusion of factors from the utility function yields

$$U = U(X_1, \ldots, X_g),$$ **1b**

with the constraint

$$\Sigma P_i X_i = \tilde{I}.$$ **4b**

Maximization of U now requires maximization of $\Sigma P_i X_i$, which when aggregated over the economy equals GNE.[1] Since

$$\Sigma P_i X_i = \Sigma P_j A_j,$$

1. Gross National Expenditure is the total value of all goods produced in a given period of time.

the corollary in aggregate is maximization of GNP.[1] The common assumption about production functions, that the marginal products of all factors are positive, leads to the corollary that factor utilization should be maximized, or that full employment is a desirable goal. Thus the conventional policy goals of maximizing GNP, achieving full employment, and in the dynamic context maximizing the rate of growth in GNP, derive analytically from the simplifying assumptions of microeconomics that were made to separate the functions of individuals as consumers of goods and suppliers of factors.

The crucial role of the simplifying assumptions as the foundation of our conventional policy goals can be demonstrated most dramatically by considering what is formally the dual[2] of the maximization problem. In the conventional approach we assume fixed the negative arguments in the utility function and maximize the remaining function **1b** which has only positive arguments (goods). This accords with the precept that hard work never hurt anyone. If instead we assume the positive arguments to be fixed then we should maximize

$$U = U(A_1, \ldots, A_f). \tag{1c}$$

This would accord with the precept that 'money', or the material affluence it brings, is not the source of happiness. Both approaches accord with the concept of efficiency in production. The former states the objective of maximizing output with given inputs, and the latter of minimizing inputs for given output. If the fixed volumes of goods are set at some target or subsistence level of consumption the problem becomes;

$$\text{maximize} \quad U = U(A_1, \ldots, A_f), \tag{1c}$$
$$\text{subject to} \quad \Sigma P_j A_j - \bar{E} = 0, \tag{4d}$$

where $\bar{E}$ is the expenditure necessary to support the postulated level of consumption.

1. Gross National Product is the total value of all factors of production employed in the economy in a given period of time.
2. The dual in this case consists of minimizing inputs for a given output rather than maximizing output for given inputs.

If $\partial U_i / \partial A_j < 0$, this requires in aggregate the minimization of $\Sigma P_j A_j$, which is GNP. Since in aggregate

$$\Sigma P_j A_j = \Sigma P_i X_i,$$

the corollary is minimization of GNE. In the dynamic context the objective would be to maximize not the rate of growth of output produced, but the rate of diminution of effort involved in production.

There is nothing incompatible about the primal and dual forms of use of the national accounts as an indicator of efficiency in production, provided that the assumptions inherent in the respective approaches are not overlooked. Maximization of GNP in constant dollars, for given factor inputs, is the corollary of minimization of GNE in constant dollars, for given product output. Considerable confusion results if the fixed quantity assumptions are not distinguished from the variable prices that bring about the identity GNP ≡ GNE. If we fix the quantities of all factor inputs and maximize GNE in constant dollars, we achieve efficient use of those fixed inputs. An increase in efficiency which raises GNE would increase GNP because it would increase the prices, not the quantities of factors. If instead we fix the output targets in quantity terms and minimize GNP in constant dollars (where the constant dollars are calculated by factor-price indices), we achieve efficient production of the fixed outputs. Increased efficiency that reduced GNP would reduce GNE because it would reduce product prices, not quantities. These two sides of the efficiency problem are exemplified by our priding ourselves each year on the production of more goods than ever before with shorter hours of work.

Achievement of either form of the objective results in achieving a position on the boundary of the transformation function. But alone or together they shed no light on the appropriate objective of the true problem of choice, the choice of the most desired position on that boundary. It is here that confusion results if we overlook the assumption that one side of the problem is assumed fixed. We could produce more if we worked harder and longer, and we could enjoy more leisure if we were satisfied with smaller volumes of goods. If we view maximization of GNE as the objective without the assumption of fixed inputs, then we involve the value judgement that it is a good thing to work harder to produce more. If we attempt to minimize GNP without the assumption of fixed output, then we involve the value judgement that it is a good thing to be satisfied with less in order to spend more time on the good things of life. Both value judgements are contentious, but some such value judgement is implicit in any use of the national accounts as a welfare objective rather than as merely an index of efficiency in production. The problem of welfare maximization is clearly deeper than anything reflected in the national accounts.

The role of value judgements

All economics is concerned with the making of choices, and rational choice necessitates the stipulation of an objective. The nature of the objective depends entirely upon the value judgements of the person stipulating it. It is important to distinguish value judgements from both behavioural assumptions and assumptions of fact. When we assume that individuals behave rationally and endeavour to maximize utility, there is no implication that such behaviour is good or bad, desirable or undesirable. Such behavioural assumptions are often reduced to truisms and are used simply to express the choice problem in a context of maximization. We assume that individuals attempt to maximize utility, and define utility as that which the individual attempts to maximize. We can similarly assume that a society attempts to maximize welfare, and define welfare as that which a society attempts to maximize. The nature of utility or welfare rests entirely on the value judgements of the individual or society concerned. Whether the consumption of alcohol, for example, is a positive or negative argument in the utility function of a particular individual depends upon his tastes or values. Whether it is a good or bad thing in the welfare function depends upon the values of the society. Since all economics is concerned with choice, choice necessitates an objective and objectives rest on value judgements, there is no such thing as value-free economics. There is, however, an important distinction between the individual values inherent in positive economics and the social values necessary for welfare economics. To assume that individuals attempt to maximize their own objectives makes the outcome of the economic system dependent on individuals' value judgements, but it says nothing about the desirability of those values. Concepts of morality, by contrast, stipulate social values that override individual choice. It is not then considered a good thing to permit freedom of individual choice in all respects. In the prohibition era in the USA the social value that the consumption of alcohol was undesirable conflicted with the fact that it was a positive argument in many individuals' utility functions. Most societies today adopt a similar attitude to narcotic drugs.

The purpose of policy is to maximize welfare. It operates by manipulating the constraints on individual choice. It is then in principle impossible to design policy, or to make any policy recommendation without implying something about the social values which govern the welfare function. It is not the business of economics to stipulate what those social values should be, but it is impossible to proceed with the business of welfare economics without some idea of what they are.

The traditional approach of economic theory, when faced with the need for facts which are not available, is to make assumptions. The theory of production rests on assumptions about the properties of production functions, the theory of consumer behaviour about the properties of utility functions. Such assumptions of fact may be tested where independent evidence is available, or their tentative validity inferred from the tested validity of the conclusions. If the internal logic of a model is rigorous then it is necessary that if the assumptions are valid the conclusions will be valid. If independent factual evidence shows the conclusions to be false, then at least one of the assumptions must have been false. If the conclusions are valid, however, it does not necessarily follow that the assumptions were valid, though repeated demonstration of the validity of the conclusions lends credence to the assumptions.

In welfare economics we need to know something about the

properties of the society's welfare function, but no clear statement of the objectives of the society is available. We are accordingly forced to make assumptions of fact concerning those properties. Such assumptions are not value judgements. To assume that a society wishes to achieve full employment is not to state that the society ought to seek full employment, any more than the assumption that production functions exhibit diminishing returns implies that diminishing returns are desirable. The conclusions of welfare economics, in so far as they constitute policy advice, are particularly vulnerable, for it is not normally possible to test the validity of either the assumptions or the conclusions against independent factual evidence. If the internal logic of the model is rigorous, then the policy implications of the conclusions will constitute good advice if the assumptions concerning objectives really do coincide with the value judgements inherent in the welfare function. It is particularly important that the assumed objective be clearly stated, for if the policy maker rejects the assumption he should have little faith in the relevance of the conclusions.

The Paretian value judgement

Following Pareto, most of the conventional theory of welfare economics rests on the assumed value judgement that if one person is better off, and no one is worse off, welfare is increased. This implies that welfare is an increasing function of individuals' utilities. Formally $W = W(U_1, \ldots, U_n)$ where $\partial W / \partial U_i > 0$ for all i. Commodities are relevant to welfare only because they are relevant to individuals' utility levels, and their welfare significance is then dependent on their utility significance. Any policy recommendation which advocates producing more of good X_1 and less of X_2, or more of X_1 by using more of factor A_1, then necessarily rests on assumptions concerning the properties not only of the welfare function, but also of the utility functions. Formally, to say that such a policy is desirable is to say that

$$dW = \sum_{\text{all } i} \frac{\partial W}{\partial U_i} \left\{ \sum_{\text{all } j} \left(\frac{\partial U_i}{\partial X_{1j}} dX_{1j} + \frac{\partial U_i}{\partial X_{2j}} dX_{2j} + \frac{\partial U_i}{\partial A_{1j}} dA_{1j} \right) \right\} > 0,$$

where dX_{1j} refers to the change in the amount of commodity X_1 going to person j. Clearly the validity of such a statement is as dependent on the assumed properties of the utility functions as it is on the assumed properties of the welfare function.

Since theoretical welfare economics is based on the Paretian value judgement, its conclusions are relevant only if that value judgement is accepted. If instead we believe that what is desirable depends upon some government's belief of what is good for the individual, rather than upon his own utility function, then the conclusions of Paretian welfare economics could not be expected to imply policies appropriate to the achievement of our social objectives.

Pure and applied welfare economics

Economics is both a pure and an applied science. As a pure science it attempts to explain and predict the outcome of the functioning of the economy; as an applied science it attempts to infer from an understanding of the working of the system some guidance as to how the outcome may be influenced.

Much of positive economics is pure in that it is concerned primarily with understanding, explaining and predicting the working of the economic system. The ability to predict makes positive economics an indispensable tool of policy formation. Market research is concerned with predicting the behaviour of consumers under various constraints (prices), and such estimates permit a firm to estimate the consequences of alternate price policies. In this way an estimate is obtained of the constraint facing the firm, and in light of this information the firm can choose a rational course of action to maximize its own objectives. Forecasting similarly enables governments and central banks to predict the consequences of alternate fiscal and monetary policies. Inherent in this process is knowledge of individual households' and firms' objective functions. On the assumption that all parties behave rationally, the ability to predict their actions presupposes knowledge of their objectives. Such knowledge can be acquired and tested by statistical means for large groups of consumers and firms, but such methods shed no light on the utility function of any particular individual.

If welfare economics could be similarly pure, and we could derive statistical knowledge of a society's welfare function, then we could predict the policy decisions that would emerge from the political process. If the welfare function is Paretian, dependent entirely upon the utility functions of individual members of the society, then statistical methods would be appropriate to deduce the basic characteristics of the objectives of individuals as citizens, just as market research yields information on their behaviour as a group of consumers. The behaviour of voters in the political process, given the constitution, lends itself to such analysis as a branch of political science. But we cannot by such means deduce what the constitution ought to be, nor can we deduce the properties of the welfare function itself. Once elected, a government pursues its objectives, one of which might be to maximize the probability of its own re-election; but the objectives of a single government do not lend themselves to statistical analysis. Individuals are far less consistent and predictable in their behaviour than groups, and there is only one government. Thus even if we accept the existing constitution as appropriate, and accept the government's objectives as a valid expression of the welfare function of the society, we cannot predict the behaviour of the government on the usual basis of assumptions of consistency and rationality combined with inferred knowledge of objectives.

For these reasons pure welfare economics, as a scientific means for explaining and predicting the behaviour of a society through the political mechanism of policy making, has met with no success. But applied welfare economics is possible. The entire body of positive economics enables us to predict the outcome resulting from alternate policies, and the use of this in welfare economics enables us to derive the appropriate policy for maximizing the achievement of any particular objective. What is the best policy in any instance depends upon the objective, the welfare function. It is then impossible for economics to yield any policy recommendations without either knowledge of, or assumptions about, the welfare function, and that function consists essentially of value judgements. The value of applied welfare economics rests on its ability to deduce appropriate policies for any particular set of social objectives, not on its inability to deduce what those objectives are or should be, nor to obviate the need for the making of value judgements for the society through the political process.

In the chapters that follow we shall be concerned with the formal analytical apparatus of welfare economics, with the derivation from this of criteria for policy, and with the properties of various political systems as means of establishing the value judgements of the society.

Part One Paretian Welfare Economics

2 The Objective and the Constraint

The basic Paretian value judgement, that welfare is increased if one person is made better off and no one worse off, was discussed in chapter 1. In order to develop the analytical apparatus of welfare maximization based on this judgement, two further related statements are needed; that welfare is decreased if one person is made worse off and no one better off, and that welfare is unchanged if no one is made either better or worse off. The formal analysis can be developed on the basis of assumptions of varying degrees of complexity. In Part One we shall restrict ourselves to the simplest set of assumptions, reserving for Part Two the modifications of the model which arise with more complex cases. Initially, we shall assume:

1. That an individual shall be considered better off if he is in a chosen position. This assumption relates the Paretian value judgement directly to the utility function. Since we define utility as that which the individual attempts to maximize, it follows that he will choose more rather than less utility. An increase in his utility can then be regarded as synonymous with his being better off.

2. That an individual's utility depends entirely on the volumes of commodities he consumes and factor services he provides. He will always be assumed to choose to consume more, or at least not less, of a commodity and to provide less, or at least not more, of a factor service. For simplicity it is assumed that no other arguments enter into the utility function.

3. That all goods are purely private[1] and that there are no

1. A purely private good is one such that the consumption of a unit of it by one person precludes its enjoyment by another. Public goods, by contrast, are simultaneously available to all. They will be introduced in chapter 7.

external economies associated with consumption or production, nor interdependence relations among utility functions.

4. That all functions are continuous, differentiable and convex.[1]

No specific assumptions need be made regarding the nature of markets while we are concerned only with the properties of optimum social states. The extent to which alternative forms of economic organization, including alternative market structures, are likely to achieve an optimum outcome will be examined in Part Two after the nature of the optimum has been defined.

The nature of the welfare function

The Paretian value judgement prescribes the form of the welfare function. If welfare increases when any single individual's utility increases, others' utility levels being unchanged, then welfare must be a positive function of every individual's utility level. Further, there can be no argument in the welfare function other than individuals' utility levels. If we consider a variable which does not enter into any individual's utility function, then a change in the value of that variable would leave all utility levels unchanged. If no one is either better off or worse off then welfare is unchanged. That variable could not influence the level of welfare and cannot therefore be an argument in the welfare function. If we consider a variable which does enter into at least one individual's utility function, and also permit it to enter the welfare function independently, then there is a potential conflict with the Paretian value judgement. If

$$W = W(U_1, \ldots, U_n, X) \quad \text{and} \quad U_1 = U_1(X, Y, \ldots),$$

then for any change in X there would be some change in Y such that the resulting change in U_1 would exactly offset the change in X in the welfare function. Formally, for any change dX in X, a change dY in Y can be calculated such that

$$dW = \frac{\partial W}{\partial X} dX + \frac{\partial W}{\partial U_1} \left(\frac{\partial U_1}{\partial X} dX + \frac{\partial U_1}{\partial Y} dY \right) = 0.$$

1. These properties rule out indivisibilities.

It follows that if

$$\frac{\partial W}{\partial X} \neq 0 \quad \text{then} \quad dU_1 = \frac{\partial U_1}{\partial X} dX + \frac{\partial U_1}{\partial Y} dY \neq 0.$$

In this case welfare would be unchanged although one individual's utility level is changed and no other individual is either better- or worse-off. Such a situation would conflict with the Paretian value judgement. Thus no variable other than individuals' utility levels can enter the welfare function independently, whether or not it also enters utility functions. The form of the Paretian welfare function is

$$W = W(U_1, \ldots, U_n),$$

where there are n individuals in the society. Each utility function must be an argument and nothing else can be.

This statement of the welfare function severely limits the form which social value judgements can take. If the welfare of society is held to depend upon the utility levels of the members of society, and upon nothing else, then the only further social value judgements to be made concern the welfare significance of each individual's utility index. In a totally egalitarian society each person's utility would count equally, though some form of interpersonal comparability of utility indices in cardinal terms would be necessary to give substance to this judgement. Alternatively it might be held that some members of society are more deserving than others, and their utility indices would be weighted more heavily in the welfare function. These are essentially distributional value judgements concerning the concept of equity prevailing in the society in question. They define the form of the welfare function, and may be stated in terms of weights attaching to individuals' utility levels. The function might then have the form $W = W(w_1 U_1, \ldots, w_n U_n)$.

There is no scope for value judgements concerning volumes of commodities or factors directly. These are the variables which determine individuals' utility levels, but the utility derived from a particular commodity depends upon the utility function, and the individual concerned determines this. The society is concerned only with the welfare significance of that utility.

In a Paretian world we cannot then have any social value judgements concerning allocation, nor any expressed in terms of goods and services. What constitutes desirable allocation is dependent in part on the welfare function, which stipulates the desired distribution of utility levels, and in part on the nature of the utility functions.

Properties of the welfare function in utility space

The formal properties of the welfare function may be stated either in terms of calculus for the general case of n persons, or in geometry for the simple case of a society of two persons. The geometric case is illustrated in Figure 1.

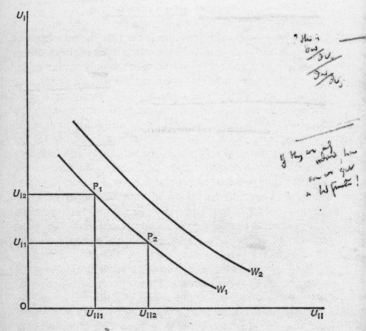

Figure 1

1. The function is $W = W(U_1, \ldots, U_n)$. When plotted geometrically the axes normally represent the utility levels of the members of the society while different levels of welfare are represented by different curves.

2. A given set of values for the utility levels yields a unique level of welfare, and a given level of welfare together with given levels of utility for all but one individual requires a unique level of utility for that individual. Geometrically this means that no welfare contour can be vertical or horizontal over any range, nor can it be downward sloping over some range and upward sloping over some other range, nor can two welfare contours meet or cross.

3. $\partial W / \partial U_i > 0$ for all i. Geometrically this means that as we move into the north-east quadrant from any point we cross welfare contours of increasing value.

4. $\partial U_i / \partial U_j < 0$ for any $i \neq j$. This follows from the last property and requires that welfare contours be downward sloping.

5. Since the utility indices are ordinal, all properties of the function are required to hold for any increasing monotonic transformation of any utility index. No significance can therefore be attached to second-order derivatives of the function, nor to curvature of the welfare contours. In particular, welfare contours are not necessarily convex to the origin for such convexity would be meaningless with ordinal utility indices.[1]

The nature of the constraint

The basic constraint on choice in the economy is the state of technology. In the static model we assume that technology is given and unchanging. Commodities can be produced only by the use of scarce factors[2] and there are maximum amounts of

---

1. Many authors draw these contours with irregular shape to indicate that curvature is quite arbitrary.

2. The scarcity of factors constitutes a constraint on which of the technically possible economic situations may be achieved. There is only so much land in the world and we cannot therefore choose a mix of factors and products in agriculture which includes more land than this. Similarly there are only so many human beings available for the labour

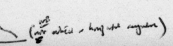

products that can be produced from any given bundle of factor inputs. The corollary of this is that there are minimum amounts of factors necessary to produce any given bundle of products. The state of technology can be stated formally as a transformation function, showing the possibilities of transforming factors A into goods X. It has the form

$$F(A_1, \ldots, A_f, X_1, \ldots, X_g) = 0,$$

where $\dfrac{\partial X_i}{\partial A_i} > 0;\quad \dfrac{\partial X_i}{\partial X_j} < 0;\quad \dfrac{\partial A_i}{\partial A_j} < 0.$

This means that if the amount of any product is increased, either the input of some factor must be increased, or the amount of some other product reduced; and if the amount of some factor is reduced either the amount of some other factor must be increased, or the amount of some product reduced.

This form of the transformation function lends itself to extensive manipulation in mathematical treatment of the subject, but for our purposes it is more convenient to break it down into its component functions for the several commodities. We are concerned with the relations that exist between product and product, factor and factor, and factor and product. For these purposes it is sufficient to have two factors and two products, the advantage of limiting ourselves to the two by two case being the ease with which the analysis can be developed in simple diagrams. We shall therefore consider the simplified form of the transformation function $F(A, B, X, Y) = 0$, where A and B are factors and X and Y products. If we stipulate the values of any three of these variables the function would yield the limiting value of the fourth, being the maximum value if the unknown is a product and the minimum value if it is a factor. If it is desired to increase the volume of any product, or reduce the volume of any factor, then there must be an

---

force, but how much work they do within the physically possible maximum will depend in part on their preference for leisure against goods. This is a property of the utility function which will concern us in the next chapter. Here we are concerned with the limits of technical possibility.

offsetting reduction in a product or increase in a factor. These 'trade-offs' can be developed for any two of the variables from the basic production functions for the two products. We shall consider first the case in which the <u>factors are given</u> and develop the 'production possibility curve' showing the possible combinations of the two products that can be produced.

The product–product trade-off

Figure 2(a) is a standard Edgeworth–Bowley box diagram. The south-west corner is the origin for product X, with the amount of factor A used in the production of X plotted along the abscissa and the amount of B plotted on the ordinate. The isoquants for X are plotted with respect to these axes and depict the contours of the production function $X = X(A, B)$. The isoquants are assumed to be smooth and convex. Isoquant X_1 shows the various combinations of A and B capable of producing quantity X_1 of X. Higher contours, X_2 and X_3, similarly depict higher quantities of X. Since both products and factors are assumed to be divisible, an isoquant could be plotted between any two others. The production function for Y, $Y = Y(A, B)$, is plotted similarly as the set of isoquants Y_1, Y_2, Y_3, drawn with respect to the north-east corner O_Y as origin. The quantity of A used in the production of Y is plotted from right to left along the abscissa, and of B from top to bottom down the ordinate. The overall width of the box depicts the fixed aggregate amount of factor A and the height the fixed amount of B. Any point within the box represents a particular allocation of A and B between X and Y. Consider the point T for example. A vertical line through T (not shown) would cut both top and bottom abscissas giving readings for the input of A to Y and X. Since input to X would be measured rightward from O_X to such a vertical line, and input to Y leftward from O_Y to the line, the aggregate input of A would exactly equal the fixed amount of A depicted by the width of the box. A horizontal line through T would similarly intersect the left and right ordinates to show the input of B to X and Y respectively, the two amounts necessarily summing to the height of the box. The outputs produced by the particular allo-

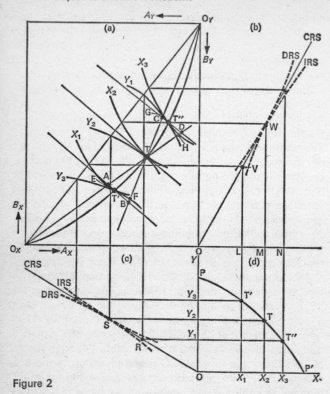

Figure 2

cation depicted by point T can be read from the values of the
X- and Y-isoquants passing through T, in this case X_2 and Y_2.

Any allocation depicted by a point in the box is possible,
but only certain allocations are optimal. If the X- and Y-isoquants intersect there must be some point nearby through which
pass both a higher X-isoquant and a higher Y-isoquant.
By reallocating factors to achieve such a point the quantities of
both products could be increased with no change in aggregate
factor input. The only positions from which such improvements
are not possible are those at which the X- and Y-isoquants do

not cross. At these points they must be tangent to each other. At T the X_2 and Y_2 isoquants are tangent and it is nowhere possible to produce both more than X_2 of X and Y_2 of Y. Similarly isoquants X_1 and Y_3 are tangent at T′ and X_3 and Y_1 at T″. The locus of such points of tangency T′TT″ shows the alternate possible optimal allocations of factors. By plotting the pairs of values for X and Y depicted by pairs of tangent isoquants on the X- and Y-axes we could derive the production possibility curve PP′ of Figure 2(d).

The above technique is completely general. In order to relate the properties of PP′ to the production functions, however, we shall make the special assumption that both production functions exhibit constant returns to scale. This means that from any initial set of values for the two inputs and product compatible with the production function, if we change the quantities of both factors by the same proportion, output will change by that proportion. A function with this property permits us to plot the entire isoquant map if we know any one isoquant. Suppose that we know isoquant X_2, and consider point T. If we increased the input of both A and B by the ratio OH/OT, we should not change the factor ratio B_X/A_X and the new point H would lie on extended ray OT. It would yield output X_3 such that $X_3/X_2 =$ OH/OT. From other points on X_2 we could similarly locate other points on X_3 by drawing the appropriate rays and extending them beyond X_2 by the same ratio. By reducing factor inputs by the ratio OE/OT we could similarly trace out the X_1 isoquant. One further important property of a CRS (constant return to scale) production function is that all the X-isoquants will have the same slope at the points where they cut the same ray.

The assumption of constant returns to scale permits us to derive the production possibility curve PP′ geometrically[1] from the contract curve T′TT″. The values of the X-isoquants will be proportional to their distances from the origin along any ray. The diagonal $O_X O_Y$ is such a ray. Mark an arbitrary distance X_1 along the abscissa of Figure 2(d), thereby pegging the scale of the axis. From X_1 draw a vertical line and extend it

1. This technique is a modification of that used by Savosnick (1958).

into Figure 2(b). Now draw a horizontal line from the point in Figure 2 (a) where the X_1 isoquant cuts the diagonal and extend it into Figure 2(b) to cut the vertical line at V. A ray OV in Figure 2(b) will now permit proportionate translations of distances along the diagonal $O_X O_Y$ of Figure 2(a) into readings on the abscissa of Figure 2(d). From the point where the X_2 isoquant cuts the diagonal we can read via W and M to X_2 in Figure 2(d), and similarly for other readings. Figure 2(c) is used to plot the output of Y. Values of Y-isoquants are proportionate to distance along the diagonal measured from O_Y. By arbitrarily marking Y_1 on the ordinate of Figure 2(d) we can locate R in Figure 2(c). The ray OR now enables us to transfer the reading Y_2 from the intersection of the Y_2 isoquant with the diagonal in Figure 2(a) via S to the ordinate of Figure 2(d). By plotting such readings from the isoquants that are tangent in Figure 2(a) we trace out the production possibility curve in Figure 2(d). The transfer of points T′, T and T″ is shown.

With the aid of this technique we can demonstrate the very important property of convexity of the production possibility curve. Select isoquants Y_1, Y_2 and Y_3 in Figure 2(a) such that the change in output $Y_3 - Y_2$ equals the change $Y_2 - Y_1$. It follows that along the ray $O_Y T$, GT = TF. Draw the common tangent to the X_2 and Y_2 isoquants through T and construct lines parallel to this through T′ and T″. Now isoquant Y_3 has this slope at F since all Y-isoquants have the same slope along the ray $O_Y T$, while isoquant X_1 has that slope at E. The constructed slope through T′ must then pass north-east of the X_1 isoquant at A and south-west of the Y_3 isoquant at B. Similarly the constructed slope through T″ passes south-west of Y_1 at C and north-east of X_3 at D. Now triangles ATB and DTC are similar because AB is parallel to CD. It follows that CT/BT = DT/AT. But CT < GT and BT > FT, while GT = FT because the Y-isoquants are equally spaced along the ray $O_Y T$. Thus we have

$$1 = \frac{GT}{FT} > \frac{CT}{BT} = \frac{DT}{AT}.$$

But $DT > HT$ and $AT < ET$. Thus

$$1 > \frac{DT}{AT} > \frac{HT}{ET}.$$

It follows that $HT < ET$, which means that the increase in output $X_3 - X_2$ is less than the increase $X_2 - X_1$. Thus as output of Y is decreased by equal amounts the output of X increases by decreasing amounts and the production possibility curve PP' in Figure 2(d) is convex.[1] *is concave is major.*

The limiting case of convexity is <u>linearity</u>. This would arise if both products used the same factor proportions, so that T', T and T'' all lay along the diagonal $O_X O_Y$. If both production functions exhibit constant returns to scale, the production possibility curve could therefore be convex, including the possible case of linearity, but could not be concave. We shall consider the cases of <u>decreasing and increasing returns</u> to scale after examining the factor–factor and factor–product trade-offs under the assumption of constant returns to scale. *pp 47–49*

The factor–factor trade-off

In this case we assume that the quantities of both products remain fixed at $\bar{X}$ and $\bar{Y}$ respectively, and examine the possibilities of reducing the input of one factor at the expense of increasing the input of the other. In Figure 3 the $\bar{X}$-isoquant is plotted with respect to axes OA, OB. The $\bar{Y}$-isoquant is plotted with respect to origin, $O_{\bar{Y}}$, which is so located that the $\bar{X}$- and $\bar{Y}$-isoquants are tangent and their respective axes parallel. O, $O_{\bar{Y}}$ now form the corners of a box of the type used in Figure 2(a) and the coordinates of $O_{\bar{Y}}$ on OA and OB locate one possible pair of inputs of A and B capable of producing $\bar{X}$ and $\bar{Y}$. If the $\bar{Y}$-isoquant is now moved round $\bar{X}$, to maintain

1. PP' is the boundary of the possible area OPP'. If a ~~straight~~ line between any two points in the feasible set nowhere passes outside the set, that set has the <u>mathematical</u> property of con<u>vex</u>ity. Thus since PP' is the outer boundary of the possible area and it is concave when viewed from the origin, the area is convex. We shall throughout refer to a curve as convex when it bounds a convex set.

tangency of the isoquants and parallel axes, alternative locations for $O\bar{Y}$ are found. In position $\bar{Y}'$ the origin is $O\bar{Y}'$, and in $\bar{Y}''$, $O\bar{Y}''$. The locus $O\bar{Y}$ so formed shows all the possible minimum combinations of A and B capable of producing $\bar{X}$ and $\bar{Y}$, the locus being read with reference to axes OA and OB. Convexity of the isoquants is sufficient to ensure that the iso-product, $\bar{X}\bar{Y}$, is convex to the origin. This is easily proved.

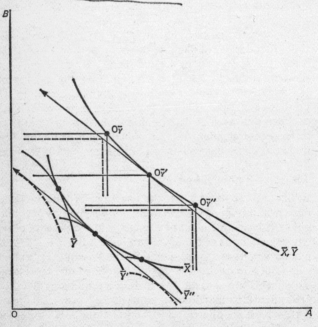

Figure 3

Starting at the tangency of $\bar{X}$ and $\bar{Y}'$ we find the point $O\bar{Y}'$. Now move $\bar{Y}'$ along a tangent to $\bar{X}$ and the locus of O_Y will be a straight line parallel to that tangent. Such positions are shown dotted in Figure 3. Since $\bar{X}$ is in fact convex, the locus $\bar{X}\bar{Y}$ lies north-east of that line on either side of $O\bar{Y}'$ and is therefore convex.

The isoproduct $\bar{X}\bar{Y}$ marks the inner boundary of possible points, for we could always be north-east of the boundary by using more of both factors inefficiently. The area of possible points is therefore convex. Since outputs of X and Y were fixed this conclusion is independent of any assumption concerning returns to scale in either the X or Y production function. All that it depends upon is convexity of the isoquants themselves.

The factor–product trade-off

In this case we assume the input of one factor, A, and one product, Y, to be fixed, and examine the possibility of increasing the output of X by increasing the input of B. In Figure 4(a) the

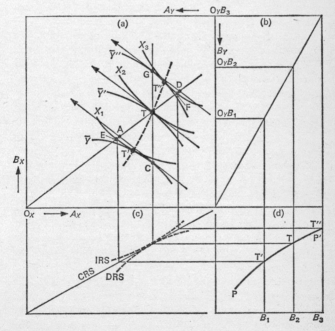

Figure 4

isoquants X_1, X_2, X_3 are plotted with respect to origin O_X. The width of the box is fixed, representing the fixed input of A. The height of the box is variable, representing the variable quantity of B. Consider the north-east corner of the box to be $O_Y B_1$. Isoquant $\bar{Y}$ drawn with respect to that origin is now tangent to X_1 at T'. As the quantity of B is increased, $O_Y B$ moves up vertically to $O_Y B_2$ and the same $\bar{Y}$-isoquant is vertically transposed together with its origin to position $\bar{Y}'$. It is now tangent to isoquant X_2 at T. A further increase in the quantity of B would move $O_Y B$ vertically to $O_Y B_3$ and $\bar{Y}$ to $\bar{Y}''$, where it is tangent to X_3 at T''. The locus of tangency points between isoquants as B is increased is T'TT''. The relevant information can be replotted in Figure 4(d). At T' we are using OB_1 of B together with the fixed $\bar{A}$ of A, to produce the fixed $\bar{Y}$ of Y together with X_1 of X. At T we have increased B to OB_2 and can produce X_2 of X with the same $\bar{A}$ of A and $\bar{Y}$ of Y.

The rays of Figures 4(b) and 4(c) permit us to plot PP' in Figure 4(d) geometrically and to examine its properties. Let us assume that the production function for X exhibits constant returns to scale. Outputs X_3, X_2, X_1 will now be in the ratio OF:OT:OE of distances along the ray O_XT. No assumption of CRS is needed for the Y production function for we do not vary the output of Y. Inputs of B can be read directly along the linear ordinate of Figure 4(a) transposed via the ray of Figure 4(b) to the abscissa of Figure 4(d).

Construct a vertical line through T. Since the Y-isoquant is transposed vertically as B is increased, points C on $\bar{Y}$, T on $\bar{Y}'$ and G on $\bar{Y}''$ are the same point on the same isoquant in different locations. Tangents to these points are therefore parallel, the slope being equal to that of X_2 at T. The X_3 isoquant has this slope at F and the tangent to $\bar{Y}''$ at G must therefore pass north-east of F at D. Similarly the tangent to $\bar{Y}$ at C passes north-east of E at A. Now assume that $B_3 - B_2 = B_2 - B_1$. It follows that GT = CT and (by similar triangles GDT and CAT) that AT = TD. But the increase in output of X from X_1 to X_2, depicted by ET along the ray, is greater than AT, while the increase from X_2 to X_3, depicted by TF along the ray, is less than TD. Since AT = TD, it follows that ET > TF. X increases by decreasing amounts as B is increased by constant amounts and PP' in Figure 4(d) must be concave from below. It is always possible to use more factor to produce less output through inefficiency, so the feasible area bounded by PP' lies south-east of the curve. This area exhibits the property of convexity.

Thus we find that if production functions exhibit constant returns to scale and isoquants are convex, the areas of feasible trade-off for product–product, factor–factor, and factor–product are all convex. We must now consider the possibility of non-constant returns to scale. We shall, however, retain the assumption of homogeneity, i.e. the isoquants will still be assumed parallel along any ray.

Decreasing returns to scale

In Figure 2(b) the ray was used to transfer distances along the diagonal $O_X O_Y$ on to the linear abscissa of Figure 2(d). If the production function for X exhibited decreasing returns to scale, isoquants spaced equidistant along a ray in Figure 2(a) would represent consecutively smaller increments of output. Transfer to the abscissa of Figure 2(d) would require not a ray in Figure 2(b) but a curve convex from below, the precise shape of the curve being governed by the rate at which returns to scale decreased. Such a curve is shown in Figure 2(b) where it is drawn tangent to the ray at W to simplify the argument although this implies a relocation for the origins of Figures 2(b) and 2(d) since the curve must pass through the origin of Figure 2(b). Relocation of the origins is inconsequential since we are concerned only with the curvature of PP', not its location.

If the readings from Figure 2(a) were transferred by use of the curve D R S in Figure 2(b) rather than the ray, points T' and T'' in Figure 2(d) would be to the left of the locations shown while T would be unaffected. The effect of decreasing returns to scale would be to intensify the convexity of the production possibility curve. The same conclusion is reached if the production function for Y has decreasing returns to scale. Using the curve D R S in Figure 2(c) we should locate both T' and T' below the positions shown, again intensifying the convexity. Similar results are obtained in Figure 4 where use of the curve DRS in Figure 4(c) rather than the ray would intensify the convexity of PP′ in Figure 4(d).

Thus the effect of decreasing returns to scale in one or both production functions is to intensify, never to offset, the convexity of the trade-offs between product–product and factor–product, while the factor–factor trade-off of Figure 3 was independent of returns to scale.

Increasing returns to scale

If the production functions exhibit increasing returns to scale, then by similar reasoning we establish the curve IRS in Figures 2(b), 2(c), and 4(c). While slightly increasing returns to scale might still leave us with convex trade-offs, significantly increasing returns could result in concavity. Increasing returns imply non-convexity of the production functions themselves, while constant or decreasing returns imply convexity.

We can therefore conclude that if all production functions are convex, the relevant trade-offs will necessarily be convex. If, however, one or more production function shows increasing returns to scale then it is possible, though not necessary, that concavities might occur in the trade-offs. Such concavities could upset the stability condition of the maximization process.

Relating the objective to the constraint

We have shown above that under the Paretian value judgement the objective, welfare, is an increasing function of individuals' utility levels, and is not directly a function of commodities or factors. The constraint, the transformation function, is a function of commodities and factors. Formally the welfare function originates in utility space while the transformation function originates in commodity space. We cannot relate one to the other in order to determine the properties of the optimum solution unless we can state them in the same variables or plot them on the same axes. It thus becomes necessary either to restate the welfare function in commodity space, or to restate the transformation function in utility space. The techniques of performing these restatements are the subject of the next chapter.

3 The Optimum Solution

In order to determine the nature of the economic situation that maximizes welfare subject to the transformation constraint, we must relate the welfare function to the transformation function. This can be done in commodity space if the welfare function is restated in terms of commodities and factors, or in utility space if the transformation function is restated in terms of achievable utility levels. We shall examine these alternative techniques in turn.

Optimization in commodity space

Restatement of the welfare function into commodity space can be undertaken either by use of calculus or geometry. In either event the medium for restatement is the set of utility functions for the individual members of the society. We shall first state the formal process in terms of calculus and then develop it in various planes geometrically.

From the welfare function $W = W(U_1, \ldots, U_n)$, for a society of n persons, and the set of n utility functions,

$$U_i = U_i(X_{1i}, \ldots, X_{gi}, A_{1i}, \ldots, A_{fi}),$$

for g goods and f factors, we can, by the function of a function rule,[1] derive

$$W = V(X_1, \ldots, X_g, A_1, \ldots, A_f).$$

This function has the following properties. For any set of values for all factors and goods it shows the maximum level

1. If W depends on U and U depends on X, then W depends on X. In this case the utility functions are substituted for the utility indices in the welfare function, and the resulting volumes of each good (factor) consumed (provided) by all persons aggregated.

of welfare attainable if the factor services and goods are optimally distributed among the members of the society. Similarly if the level of welfare to be achieved and the values for all but one of the factors and goods are specified, the function yields the necessary value for the remaining factor or good, being the minimum necessary volume for a good and the maximum possible volume for a factor. It is a minimum value for a good because with less of the good we could not achieve any utility levels yielding the prescribed level of welfare, but with more of the good we could achieve that level even with suboptimal distribution.

The process of deriving the welfare function in commodity space and the relevant properties of that function are more clearly seen in the geometric techniques, and to facilitate the development of these we shall make the simplifying assumptions that there are only two persons, two goods and two factors. In examining the trade-offs in the constraint we found that with given technology it was possible to have more of one good, or provide less of one factor, only if we made do with less of some good or provided more of some factor. We accordingly developed the trade-offs for product against product, factor against factor and factor against product. These specified the possible technical substitution of one for the other. In the welfare function we are similarly concerned with trade-offs but now with substitutions that leave us indifferent. The constraint tells us that if we have less of one good it is possible to have a certain amount more of some other, whether we should be better off or worse off as a result of the change. The objective tells us that if we made do with less of one good we should need a certain amount more of some other in order to be as well off, whether or not it would be technically possible to effect such a change. The three indifference trade-offs, concerning product–product, factor–factor, and factor–product will be developed in turn.

The product–product indifference trade-off

In this case we shall assume that the amount of each factor provided by each person is fixed. Each individual utility function can then be depicted by a conventional indifference map on axes for the two goods X and Y. Each indifference curve represents a level of utility and curves further from the origin represent higher levels of utility. The curves are assumed to be downward sloping and convex to the origin. Since utility itself is not assumed to be cardinally measurable, we can attach any increasing series of numbers to the indifference curves of a particular individual's map. Differences and ratios between these arbitrary numbers are without any significance, for they can be adjusted to any values we like by changing the numbers. Only the ordinal properties of those numbers are significant; they are used to depict more or less, but not how much more or less. Formally, the series constitutes an index of utility and the assumption of ordinal utility restricts us to only those properties of the index that hold for any increasing monotonic transformation.

Let us suppose that we have selected a particular set of numbers to represent the utility levels of each individual. These indices U_I and U_{II} then constitute the scales for the axes of Figure 1(p. 36). The value judgements of the society are represented by the contours of the welfare function. The contour W_1 tells us that society is indifferent among position P_1, P_2, and all other points on the contour. Any position on W_2 is preferred to all positions on W_1. Indifference between P_1 and P_2 states that a situation in which person I is on his indifference curve U_{I2} and person II on his U_{II1}, is considered neither more nor less desirable than a situation in which I achieves U_{I1} and II, U_{II2}.

Position P_1 is uniquely associated with one indifference curve for each individual. From these we can derive a 'community indifference curve' in commodity space showing the various combinations of X and Y that would make it possible to achieve that pair of utility levels. In Figure 5 the indifference curve U_{I2} is plotted on axes depicting commodities X and Y. Indifference curve U_{II1} is similarly plotted, but with respect to origin O_{II}, that origin being so located that the two X-axes are parallel, as are the Y-axes, and the two indifference curves tangent. The two origins now form the corners of a box with width equal to an aggregate amount of X and height equal to an aggregate amount of Y that would, if distributed as indicated by the point of tangency between the two indifference curves, enable us to achieve utility levels U_{I2} and U_{III}.

Indifference curve U_{III} can now be moved round U_{I2}, always maintaining parallel axes and tangent indifference

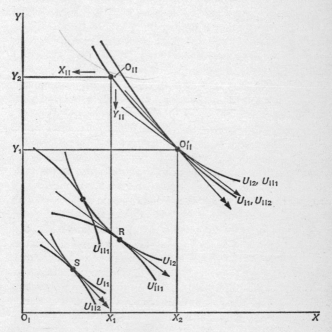

Figure 5

curves. The locus of O_{II} as this operation is performed traces out curve U_{I2}, U_{III}, the coordinates of which with respect to O_I show the alternate combinations of X and Y that would support utility levels U_{I2}, U_{III}. Position O'_{II}, for example, shows that X_2 of X and Y_1 of Y would be just as good as X_1 of X and Y_2 of Y if both were so distributed as to yield U_{I2} and U_{III}. If both indifference curves are convex the community indifference curve U_{I2}, U_{III} must be convex. The proof of this proposition is the same as the proof of the convexity of $\bar{X}$, $\bar{Y}$ in Figure 3, only here we are concerned with indifference curves and in Figure 3 with isoquants.

The entire *curve* U_{I2}, U_{III} of Figure 5 is thus derived from the *point* P_1 of Figure 1. Point P_2 could similarly be translated into curve U_{I1}, U_{II2} of Figure 5. Since points P_1 and P_2 are on the same welfare contour it follows that any point on U_{I2}, U_{III} represents a combination of X and Y which, if distributed so as to yield U_{I2}, U_{III}, would be just as good as any point on U_{I1}, U_{II2} distributed to yield U_{I1}, U_{II2}. While both community indifference curves are necessarily downward sloping and convex there is no reason why they should not intersect. Point O'_{II} exists on U_{I2}, U_{III} because the box $O_I X_2 O'_{II} Y_1$ accommodated indifference curves U_{I2}, U_{III} tangent at R. As we move U'_{III} round U_{I2} to trace out the community indifference curve, its slope at O'_{II} must be the same as the slope of the common tangent to the indifference curves at R. Now the same box might just accommodate indifference curves U_{I1}, U_{II2} tangent at S. Point S would correspond with P_2 while R corresponds with P_1. In that case point O'_{II} would also be a point on community indifference curve U_{I1}, U_{II2} described by moving U_{II2} round U_{I1}. The slope of U_{I1}, U_{II2} at O'_{II} would then be the same as the slope of the common tangent to the indifference curves at S. With no special assumptions about the utility function there is no reason why the slope of the common tangent at R should equal that of the common tangent at S. If these slopes differ, then so do the slopes of U_{I2}, U_{III} and U_{I1}, U_{II2} at O'_{II}, at which point the two community indifference curves would intersect.

The welfare contour in commodity space will depict the minimum volumes of X and Y that permit the achievement of W_1. The curve U_{I2}, U_{III} south-east of O'_{II} shows combinations of X and Y that permit achievement of P_1 on W_1, but it does not show *minimum* combinations that can achieve W_1, for U_{I1}, U_{II2} shows smaller combinations of X and Y that can achieve W_1 at P_2. If the community indifference curves cross then the portions of curves showing the larger volumes of X and Y are not part of the welfare contour. For each point on W_1 in Figure 1 there will be a community indifference curve in Figure 5. The welfare contour W_1 in commodity space will be the boundary or envelope of that entire set of curves. The contour W_2 of Figure 1, representing a higher level of welfare, can similarly be restated as a contour in commodity space, being the envelope of the entire set of community indifference curves generated by all points on W_2 in Figure 1.

Properties of the welfare function in commodity space

Our assumptions, that X and Y are goods, that individuals always choose to have more rather than less of any good and that the welfare function is Paretian, ensure that the contours of the welfare function are downward sloping and non-intersecting. Each community indifference curve is downward sloping and convex, but the various curves generated from the points on a particular welfare contour in utility space might intersect. These differences between the properties of the community indifference curves and the envelope of a set of such curves generated from one welfare contour are a source of some confusion. The curves might cross, but each is necessarily convex; the envelopes cannot cross, but they need not be convex.

Non-convexity of the welfare contour is a troublesome possibility. It can be ruled out by constraining the value judgements that a society is assumed to make, but in order to appreciate the nature of the restriction imposed, it is first necessary to understand how non-convexity can arise. In Figure 6 consider the bundle of goods Q_1 and the box with corners O, Q_1. Indifference curves for party I (U_{I1}, U_{I2}) are plotted with reference to origin O and those for party II with reference to origin Q_1. Points of tangency between indifference curves would form a contract curve (not shown) of which P_1 would be one point. Suppose the distributional value judgements to be such that P_1 is the chosen distribution on that contract curve. The pair of utility levels (U_{I2}, U_{II1}) at P_1 coincides with point P_1 of Figure 1. Now consider the bundle Q_2, which similarly defines a box containing a contract curve and assume that point P_2 is the chosen distribution on that curve. It yields utility levels $U_{\text{II}1}$, $U_{\text{II}2}$ which coincides with point P_2 of Figure 1. Note that the utility levels derived from P_1 are not attainable with Q_2, nor those derived from P_2 attainable with Q_1. Finally suppose that, as in Figure 1, the points P_1 and P_2 lie on the same welfare contour in utility

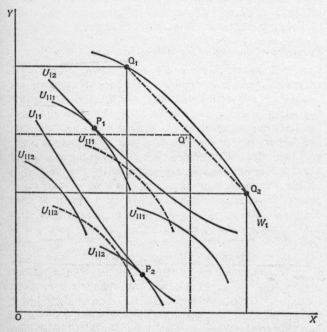

Figure 6

space. Q_1 and Q_2 must therefore lie on the same welfare contour in commodity space. Now consider the point Q' which is the midpoint of a straight line joining Q_1 and Q_2. It describes the box shown by dotted lines. With the bundle of goods Q' it is not possible to achieve either the pair of utility levels $U_{\text{II}1}$, $U_{\text{II}2}$ or the pair $U_{\text{I}2}$, $U_{\text{II}1}$. If no pair of utility levels achievable with Q' is judged as good as either of these then all such achievable pairs will lie below the W_1 contour of Figure 1. In commodity space the bundle Q' will therefore lie below W_1 in Figure 6. W_1 must therefore pass north-east of Q', although passing through Q_1 and Q_2. The contour W_1 would then be concave.

Concavity of the welfare function in commodity space can be ruled out only by assumption about the value judgements inherent in the welfare function. It is sufficient to assume that welfare preferences are non-troughed along any line segment between two points in commodity space that yield equal welfare, but the significance of this assumption must be explained to be appreciated.[1] Let us begin at position P_1 at which party I receives X_I of X and Y_I of Y and party II, X_{II} of X and Y_{II} of Y. These volumes of commodities with this distribution yield utility levels U_{I2}, U_{III}. The welfare associated with such a position can be expressed either in terms of the basic welfare function $W = W(U_{I2}, U_{III})$ or in terms of the derived form $W = V(X_I, X_{II}, Y_I, Y_{II})$. Movement to position P_2 involves changing the quantity of each commodity going to each party. Let the changes be dX_I, dX_{II}, dY_I, dY_{II}. Welfare at P_2 can then be expressed in terms of the derived form of the welfare function as

$$W^* = V(X_I + dX_I, X_{II} + dX_{II}, Y_I + dY_I, Y_{II} + dY_{II}).$$

These changes define a line segment from the starting point of P_1 in the four-dimensional space X_I, X_{II}, Y_I, Y_{II}. If welfare at P_1 equals welfare at P_2 then $W = W^*$. Now consider a position P', representing the utility levels that would be achieved if we moved from P_1 only half-way to P_2, that is if the change in the quantity of each good going to each party were half that necessary to move from P_1 to P_2. Welfare at P' would be

$$W' = V(X_1 + dX_I/2, X_{II} + dX_{II}/2, Y_I + dY_I/2, Y_{II} + dY_{II}/2).$$

The assumption that welfare preferences are non-troughed along a line segment means that if welfare at the starting point P_1 is W and at the terminus of the line segment, (i.e. at point

1. A more general statement of the sufficient conditions for this assumption to be satisfied is contained in the appendix to this chapter.

P_2) is W^*, and $W = W^*$, then welfare at a point halfway along that line segment (i.e. W') is not less than W or W^*. Now the position P' would be achievable with the aggregate bundle of X and Y depicted by Q' in Figure 6, since Q' is the midpoint of the line joining Q_1 and Q_2. Since Q' can yield W', while $W' \geqslant W = W^*$, Q' cannot lie on a lower welfare contour than Q_1 or Q_2. The contour W_1 in Figure 6 would then be convex. In simple language we can state the assumption in the following way. If adverse changes in the quantities of commodities going to one person are judged to be just offset in welfare terms by certain changes in quantities going to another person, then changes of half that extent for the first person would be at least offset by changes of half that extent for the other person.

The factor–factor indifference trade-off

Derivation of the welfare function in factor space is completely analogous to its derivation in product space. In this case we assume that the amount of each product going to each person is fixed, so that their utility levels are dependent on the volumes of factor services they provide. Our assumption that individuals would always choose to provide less rather than more factor services means that indifference curves closer to the origin in factor space depict higher levels of utility, while the assumption of convexity of utility functions means that the indifference curves will appear concave. In Figure 7 two indifference curves U_{I1} and U_{I2} are plotted with reference to origin O_I on axes $O_I A$ and $O_I B$, A and B being the two factors. Indifference curves for party II are similarly plotted with reference to O_{II}. Consider the point R, the coordinates of which show the volume of each factor provided by each person. With the given volumes of products going to each person, the utility levels achieved would be U_{I2}, U_{II1}. Point R thus coincides with P_1 in Figure 1. We can now move the origin O_{II} so as to maintain parallel axes and tangency of the indifference curves. The locus of O_{II} as this operation is performed traces out the community indifference curve U_{I2}, U_{II1}. The *point* P_1 in Figure 1 then translates into a community indifference *curve* in Figure 7, just as it did in the product space of Figure 5. Since both indifference curves are convex the community curve will be convex (all will appear concave when viewed from the origin since the origin is within the set of points bounded by the curve, the set being all points capable of yielding the utility levels shown). As before, point S shows an alternate distribution of the same aggregate volumes of factor services, and would yield utility levels

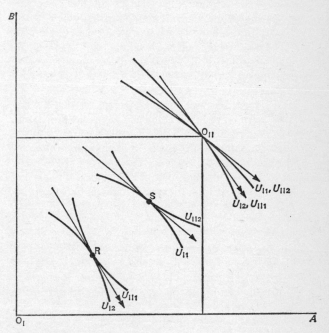

Figure 7

U_{II1}, U_{II2}. Point S thus represents P_2 in Figure 1. The locus of O_{II}, maintaining tangency of U_{I1}, U_{II2}, is the community indifference curve U_{I1}, U_{II2}. Since the slope of the indifference curves at R need not equal that at S, these two community indifference curves might well cross. One represents P_1 in Figure 1 and one P_2. Community indifference curves could similarly be constructed for all other points on the welfare contour W_1 in Figure 1. The welfare contour in factor space will be the envelope of this entire set of community indifference curves, just as it was in product space. In factor space, however, the envelope will encompass those portions of the community indifference curves that are farthest out from the origin, whereas in product space it encompassed the portions closest to the origin. The welfare contour in product space showed the *minimum* volume of commodities that, if optimally distributed, could enable us to achieve the level of welfare in question. In factor space it shows the *maximum* volumes of factor services that could be provided, if the work load were optimally distributed, and still permit achievement of the relevant level of welfare.

In product space we made a special assumption (that welfare preferences are non-troughed along any line segment in commodity space) to rule out non-convexity of the welfare contours. The same assumption with respect to factor space rules out concavity by the same reasoning. Contours of the welfare function in the factor space will then be convex (i.e. appear concave when viewed from the origin) and contours closer to the origin will represent higher levels of welfare.

The factor–product indifference trade-off

In this case we assume that the volume of factor B provided by each person and the volume of Y consumed by him are fixed. Utility is then dependent on the volume of factor A provided and the quantity of good X consumed. Indifference curves for the two parties on axes for A and X are shown in Figure 8. The indifference curves are upward sloping in this case because the individual would rather provide less of the factor but consume more of the good. By moving one person's indifference curve round the other the community indifference curves are traced out in the usual manner. The welfare contour will again be the envelope of the set of community indifference curves derived from the points on one welfare contour in utility space. The usual assumption of non-troughed welfare preferences ensures convexity of the welfare contours. They will appear convex when viewed from the axis depicting

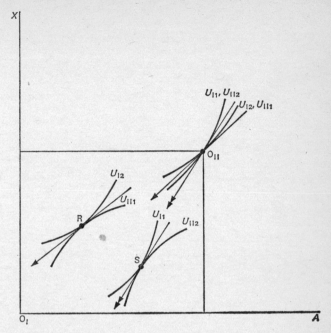

Figure 8

factor A. Increasing the quantity of X increases welfare, while increasing the quantity of A reduces welfare.

Relating objective to constraint

Once the welfare function has been restated in commodity space, its maximization subject to the transformation constraint is a simple matter using conventional techniques. Given the welfare function

$$W = W(U_1, \ldots, U_n),$$

and the utility functions

$$U_i = U_i(X_{1i}, \ldots, X_{gi}, A_{1i}, \ldots, A_{fi}),$$

the welfare function can be restated as

$$W = V(X_{11}, \ldots, X_{1n}, \ldots, X_{g1}, \ldots, X_{gn}, A_{11}, \ldots, A_{1n}, \ldots,$$
$$A_{f1}, \ldots, A_{fn}).$$

Maximization of this function subject to the transformation constraint

$$F(\sum_{i=1}^{n} x_{1i}, \ldots, \sum_{i=1}^{n} x_{gi}, \sum_{i=1}^{n} A_{1i}, \ldots, \sum_{i=1}^{n} A_{fi}) = 0$$

yields the specification of the welfare optimum in terms of the amount of each factor to be provided by each person and the volume of each good to be consumed by each person.

The nature of the welfare optimum can be more clearly seen

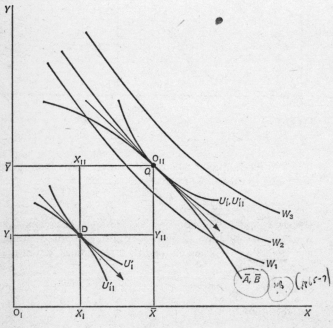

Figure 9

geometrically by examining each plane of the two persons, two factors, two goods case. Figures 9, 10, and 11 depict the opti-

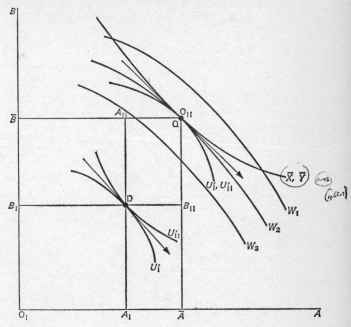

Figure 10

mum position in the XY, AB, AX planes respectively. The AY, BX, and BY planes are analogous to the AX plane. At the optimum position party I provides A_I of A and B_I of B, and consumes X_I of X and Y_I of Y. Similarly the volumes for party II are A_{II}, B_{II}, X_{II} and Y_{II}. The total volume $\bar{A}$ of A provided is given by

$$A_I + A_{II} = \bar{A}$$

and similarly

$$B_I + B_{II} = \bar{B}, \quad X_I + X_{II} = \bar{X} \quad \text{and} \quad Y_I + Y_{II} = \bar{Y}.$$

In Figure 9 the transformation function $\bar{A}$, $\bar{B}$ is the curve derived in Figure 2(d), the corresponding box of Figure 2(a) having dimensions $\bar{A}$, $\bar{B}$. The welfare contours W_1, W_2, W_3 are as derived from Figure 5, the relevant factor inputs being

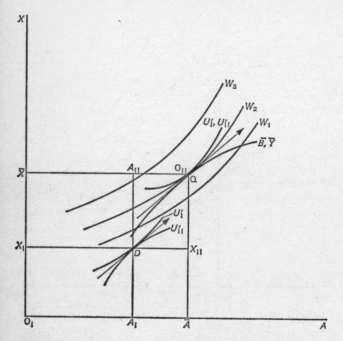

Figure 11

A_I, A_II, B_I and B_II. The appropriate assumptions discussed earlier that ensured convexity of the transformation function and welfare function, result in a single point Q at which a welfare contour is tangent[1] to the transformation function. This point has coordinates showing the volumes of X and Y, $\bar{X}$ and $\bar{Y}$, that permit achievement of the highest possible level

1. Corner solutions are possible at which either $X = 0$ or $Y = 0$ but we shall not concern ourselves with them at this stage.

of welfare given the constraint. The welfare contour W_2 is the envelope of a set of community indifference curves derived from the welfare contour of Figure 1. Point Q will therefore be a point on some community indifference curve U'_I, U'_{II} and this curve will be tangent to the welfare contour at Q. Letting Q be the origin O_{II} of a box $O_I \bar{X} O_{II} \bar{Y}$ permits us to plot the indifference curves U'_I, U'_{II} which will be tangent at a point D (see Figure 5). The coordinates of D, X_I, X_{II}, Y_I, Y_{II} show the welfare maximizing distribution of X and Y.

Figure 10 is similarly derived from Figures 3 and 7. The isoproduct $\bar{X}\bar{Y}$ is taken from Figure 3 and the welfare contours W_1, W_2, and W_3 were derived in Figure 7. Again our assumptions ensure tangency at Q, showing that the optimum way to produce $\bar{X}$, $\bar{Y}$ is by using $\bar{A}$, $\bar{B}$. The community indifference curve U'_I, U'_{II} is tangent to W_2 at Q and the box $O_I \bar{A} O_{II} \bar{B}$ contains indifference curves $U'_I U'_{II}$ tangent at D showing the optimum distribution of the provision of factor services A_I, A_{II}, B_I, B_{II}. Figure 11 is similarly derived from Figures 4 and 8, the point D showing the optimum distribution of input, A_I, A_{II} and output X_I, X_{II}.

It is important to remember that Figures 9, 10 and 11 do not exist independently; they represent three cross-sections of one multi-dimensional maximization situation. The curves in each diagram have the solutions of the others as parameters. The indifference curves in Figure 9, for example, hold only if the factor inputs are as shown in Figure 10, and the indifference curves in Figure 10 hold only if consumption levels are as shown in Figure 9. Similarly the transformation function of Figure 9 holds only for the aggregate factor inputs shown in figure 10, while the isoproduct of Figure 10 holds only for the commodity outputs shown in Figure 9.

The simultaneous fulfilment of all the conditions shown in Figures 9, 10 and 11 (together with the corresponding conditions in the AY, BX and BY planes), and the assumption that all functions are convex, constitute both necessary and sufficient conditions for the maximization of welfare. They are sufficient because it is nowhere possible to adjust any variable so as to achieve a higher welfare contour. They are necessary because if tangency did not exist at Q in any of the diagrams it would be possible to adjust the variables so as to achieve greater welfare. In Figure 9 this would involve the production of more of one good and less of the other, and in Figure 11 it would involve the use of more (less) of a factor to produce more (less) of the good.

If a situation exists in which the tangency conditions hold in all but one (or more) of the diagrams, but do not hold in one (or more), then the readings from the diagrams in which tangency holds are not valid for the welfare optimum.[1] This results from the interdependence of the planes. If tangency did not exist at Q in Figure 9, for example, but did exist in Figures 10 and 11, the very process of changing the combination of products in Figure 9 to achieve tangency would change the parameters, and accordingly the curves, of Figures 10 and 11 so that tangency would not then exist there.

Optimization in utility space

Just as it was possible to restate the welfare function, that originated in utility space, into commodity space by use of utility functions and then relate it to the transformation function, so it is possible to restate the transformation function into utility space and then relate it to the welfare function. Again the restatement is performed via the medium of individual utility functions. In our simplified case with two factors, two goods and two persons, the process of restatement is different because of the differing number of dimensions of the two spaces. Utility space has one dimension for each individual's utility, and our simple case is therefore depicted in a single plane diagram. Commodity space has a dimension for each factor and one for each good, resulting in four dimensions with six different cross-sections. Restatement of the welfare function into commodity space therefore increased the number of dimensions from two to four, while restatement of the transformation function into utility space involves reducing the number of dimensions from four to two.

Let us begin, as before, by assuming that the volume of each

1. We shall return to such cases in chapter 6 where we discuss second-best optima.

factor provided by each person is fixed. This permits us to plot an indifference map for each person as a plane cross-section of the utility function on axes X and Y. Fixity of aggregate factor volumes similarly permits us to use the plane cross-section of the transformation function on axes X and Y. The transformation function TT of Figure 12 is as derived in Figure 2. Any point Q constitutes the origin for a box O_I, $\bar{X}$, Q, $\bar{Y}$, and the indifference maps for the two parties can be plotted in this box with respect to their respective origins. The locus of tangency points between indifference curves, the contract curve CC, shows the alternate ways of distributing the bundle of goods Q so that it is impossible to make both parties simultaneously better off. Each point of tangency is associated with a level of utility for each person, and these pairs of utility levels (U_{I1}, U_{II3}; U_{I2}, U_{II2}; U_{I3}, U_{II1}) can be plotted on axes U_I, U_{II} to form a utility possibility curve. Other points on TT can similarly be replotted as utility possibility curves. Thus just as each point on the welfare function of Figure 1 yielded a community indifference curve in Figure 5, so each point on the transformation function of Figure 12 yields a utility possibility curve. Since the utility indices are ordinal, the only known property of each utility possibility curve is that it is downward sloping. Each curve shows the alternate maximum pairs of utility levels achievable, if the parties provide the assumed levels of factor services and a particular combination of commodities is produced. Alternate positions on the curve result from varying the distribution of goods between the parties. The outer envelope of the set of utility possibility curves yielded from all points on the curve TT in Figure 12 shows the alternate maximum pairs of utility-levels that could be achieved if we were free to vary the combination of goods produced as well as their distribution, while being still bound by the assumed factor inputs.

Each possible set of assumptions about the volume of each factor provided by each person will yield a different curve TT in Figure 12, different indifference maps, a different set of utility possibility curves and a different envelope. The outer boundary of the infinite set of such envelopes will be the transformation function in utility space, sometimes called the utility possibility frontier.

The same frontier could alternately have been developed by assuming initially that the amount of each commodity consumed by each person was fixed and plotting the analogue of Figure 12 on axes A and B as in Figure 3. Each point on the isoproduct would then yield a utility possibility curve and the

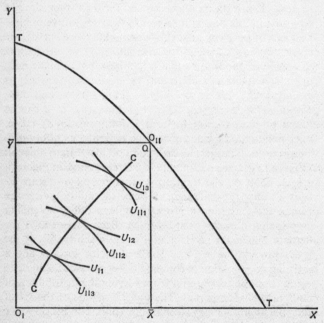

Figure 12

set of curves an envelope. By varying the assumptions about the consumption of goods different envelopes would result, the outer boundary of these being the utility possibility frontier. The same technique beginning with the assumption that the volume of one factor provided by each person was fixed, together with the volume of one good consumed, would again have resulted in the same frontier.

That these alternate routes result in the same utility frontier follows from the fact that they are based on the same assumptions. Whether we begin by permitting only the distribution of fixed volumes of commodities to vary, then permit the combination of commodities to vary, and finally permit the factor inputs to vary; or alternatively relax the fixity assumptions in any other order, the frontier represents the boundary of attainable utility levels when all variables in the transformation function are variable both in aggregate and in distribution.

Once the utility possibility frontier is established, it can be superimposed on the welfare function of Figure 1. Since the axes are ordinal utility levels, it is not easy to establish properties such as convexity which would ensure that there is one unique point at which the utility possibility frontier is tangent to a welfare contour, but if such a unique point exists it would represent the welfare optimum. The assumptions which ensured convexity of all relevant functions in commodity space did guarantee a unique solution, however, and if these same assumptions hold we can be sure of a unique solution in utility space. This follows from the fact that mere restatement of a problem from one space to another cannot change its properties. If, then, there were a single determinate welfare optimum when the problem was analysed in commodity space, there must be a unique solution when the same problem is analysed in utility space.

The single point of tangency between a welfare contour and the utility possibility frontier indicates the level of welfare achievable and the corresponding level of utility achieved by each person. The corresponding volumes of factor inputs and goods consumed are read from the particular point on the utility possibility frontier. Any point on that frontier is also a point on one of the envelopes it bounds, and a point on the envelope is also a point in one of the utility possibility curves it bounds. The chosen point thus identifies a particular point on a particular utility possibility curve for each of the routes by which the frontier could have been established. Each of those curves has associated with it a set of parameters, and that entire set defines the volume of each factor service provided by, and the volume of each commodity consumed by, each person. It is impossible for the parameters from various approaches to be incompatible for points on the frontier, for this would imply that the solution is not unique.

The respective advantages of commodity and utility space

The formal analysis of the welfare maximization model has been presented in both commodity space and utility space, because both spaces are used in the literature, although the relations between them are rarely discussed explicitly. The choice of space in which to develop a model deserves careful consideration, for each has its advantages. Which should be chosen depends upon the focus of emphasis in the problem under analysis.

Commodity space has the advantage that its dimensions are tangible, measurable and cardinal. The transformation function is at home in commodity space, and where the subject under discussion is concerned primarily with the possible, commodity space is normally the better medium in which to work. Convexity can be established and is meaningful while the first- and second-order conditions of optimization can be explored with manageable cardinal functions. We shall accordingly use commodity space in the next chapter in developing the Paretian conditions of optimization. Exchange takes place among commodities and factors, and price ratios are easily depicted by slopes in commodity space. Where, then, the welfare implications of various market structures are under analysis, commodity space is a convenient medium in which to work. The optimality of perfect competition will be examined in this way.

Utility space is ordinal, and properties of convexity, first- and second-order conditions and the significance of slopes are either meaningless or treacherous to work with. However, the Paretian welfare function originates in utility space and where the basic value judgements concerning the objectives of the society are under examination, utility space is the appropriate medium. While problems of resource allocation and exchange are more readily handled in commodity space, problems connected with distribution are more apparent in utility space.

Utility space also has the advantage that a single model can depict a wide range of alternate particular problems. The utility possibility curve can arise with various combinations of fixed and variable inputs and outputs. The fundamental welfare considerations of a wide range of situations calling for policy decisions can therefore be explored in utility space with the aid of a single diagram. The compensation principle will be examined in this space, for we are then concerned with the validity of the principle of compensation rather than the particular case of who is being compensated for exactly what.

Whichever space is chosen in a particular context it is important to remember that both are involved. The focus of attention on the commodity dimensions of the transformation function should not lead us to overlook the fact that even when working in commodity space we are concerned with a welfare function that originates in utility space. Similarly, in utility space we are working with a constraint that originates in commodity space. In both cases the ability to work in a single space is achieved only by a restatement of either objective or constraint, and that restatement involves the properties of utility functions. This critical role of utility functions should never be overlooked, for while it is obvious that if the purpose of economic activity is the creation of utility then the relationship between utility and commodities is crucial, it is a common pitfall to state conclusions and even to make policy recommendations without a clear statement of the assumptions about both the value judgements inherent in the welfare function and the properties of utility functions on which any such conclusions necessarily rest.

Appendix to Chapter Three

Convexity of the welfare function

In order to establish convexity of the welfare function in commodity space we assumed that welfare preferences were non-troughed along a line segment in commodity space. While simple and sufficient for our purpose this assumption was unsatisfactory in that welfare preferences do not exist in the first instance in commodity space, they exist in utility space. We must here examine the basic properties of utility functions and the welfare function in utility space that will be sufficient to ensure that the welfare function in commodity space has the required properties.

Utility is assumed to be ordinal while factors and commodities are cardinal. The normal assumption that indifference curves or surfaces are convex is meaningful, because utility here is a constant and all variables cardinal. It would not, however, be meaningful to speak of a convex function in any cross-section involving utility as a variable, for utility is an ordinal index and subject to any increasing monotonic transformation. Any set of increasing numbers is as good as any other in designating ordinal utility.[1] There is in principle an infinite set of specific functions, each being an increasing monotonic transformation of all others in the utility dimension, and any one of these is as good as any other in representing an ordinal utility function. If these are plotted on linear axes, including a linear axis for the utility index, some will appear convex in cross-sections involving utility as a variable and some will not. It is always possible to establish such apparent con-

---

1. It is accordingly meaningless to speak of decreasing marginal utility if utility is ordinal.

vexity by appropriate increasing monotonic transformation, but such convexity is only apparent for particular indices and is not a real property of the utility function itself.

Now the utility indices of the several persons in the society are the dimensions of the utility space in which the welfare function is postulated. If we subject any utility function to an increasing monotonic tranformation in the utility dimension we subject that dimension of utility space to the same transformation for purposes of plotting the welfare function. In this way monotonic transformations of utility indices cancel out when we restate the welfare function in commodity space.[1] When we select a particular index for each utility function and use these as the dimensions of the welfare function, we can plot the welfare contours in commodity space. If we select other utility indices instead, the apparent changes in the utility functions are offset by converse apparent changes in the welfare function, and the welfare contours in commodity space are unaffected. Any monotonic transformation of the utility functions which makes them appear more convex will make the welfare function in utility space appear less convex and vice versa. By monotonic transformation of utility indices it is always possible to make utility functions appear convex at the expense of apparent nonconvexity of the welfare function in utility space, or to make the welfare function appear convex at the expense of apparent non-convexity of the utility functions. Such manipulations will in no way affect the welfare function in commodity space.

If it is possible to find a utility index for each person such that each utility function appears everywhere convex and simultaneously the welfare function when plotted on axes depicting those same utility indices also appears convex, then it must be true that welfare preferences are non-troughed along a line segment in commodity space, and accordingly that the welfare contours are convex in commodity space. If such a set of indices exists then the welfare contours in commodity space will be convex no matter what indices are in fact chosen. It is

1. We are of course left with the ordinal nature of welfare, but that is not our concern at the moment.

then sufficient, though not necessary, to establish convexity of the welfare contours in commodity space to assume that the value judgements inherent in the welfare function are such that such a set of utility indices exists.

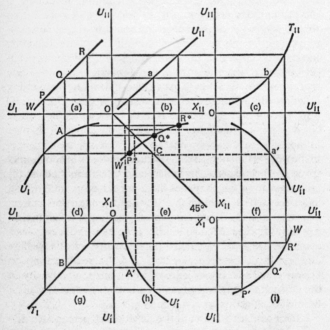

Figure 13

These propositions are illustrated in Figure 13. Segment (a) shows a contour of the welfare function on axes representing certain indices of utility for two parties. Segment (b) shows the utility level achieved by party II for different levels of consumption of X, all other goods consumed by him and all factor services provided by him being constant. Segment (d) similarly shows the utility level of party I as a function of his consumption of X. Segment (e) shows the welfare contour in commodity space corresponding to the contour in utility space of segment (a). Point Q in (a) has coordinates giving the utility levels for the two parties, and points A in (d) and a in (b) enable us to read the levels of consumption required to yield these utility levels, these commodity volumes being the co-ordinates of Q* in (e). Points P* and R* are similarly derived from points P and R. It is readily apparent that if one of the curves in (a) (b) or (d) appears convex and none concave, the curve in (e) is convex. Cross-sections involving other factors or commodities than X have similar properties, from which we can infer that in hyperspace the welfare function in commodity space is convex if the utility and welfare functions simultaneously appear convex.

The utility index U_{II} is transformed into U'_{II} by the increasing monotonic transformation of segment (c). With the aid of this and the 45° ray of segment (e) we can replot the utility curve for party II with respect to index U'_{II}. Point a in segment (b) becomes a' of segment (f) by readings via b in (c) and C in (e). The effect of the transformation is that while the utility curve appeared linear in (b) it appears convex in (f). Segment (g) similarly permits us to subject the index U_I to transformation into U'_I, the proportional transformation shown having no effect on curvature. In segment (i) the welfare contour of (a) is replotted on axes U'_I, U'_{II}, point Q being read through a, b and a' to Q' for party II and through A, B and A' to Q' for I, and points P and R similarly replotted as P' and R'. It is readily apparent that the transformation of U_{II} into U'_{II} which made the utility function for II appear convex has simultaneously made the welfare function appear concave. From (i) we can again replot the welfare function in commodity space in segment (e) following the dotted lines. The transformation that affected the apparent convexity of the utility function and welfare function in utility space has no effect on the welfare function in commodity space.

Since the same properties hold for all dimensions of distributed commodity space it follows that if there is some set of increasing utility indices that would result in the utility and welfare functions all simultaneously appearing convex, the welfare function in commodity space would be convex and would retain its convexity unchanged for all increasing monotonic transformations of utility indices.

4 The Paretian Optimum

The concept of the Paretian optimum has come to have a very special, and somewhat misleading, meaning in economics. There are three aspects of optimum performance of an economic system, associated respectively with the three basic functions (the transformation function, the utility function and the welfare function). The unique optimum economic situation requires perfect performance in all three respects, but the term 'Paretian Optimum' has come to mean the simultaneous fulfilment of the first two regardless of the third. There are accordingly an infinite number of Paretian optima, any one of which is commonly called *an* optimum, while *the* optimum is sometimes distinguished by calling it the *optimum optimorum* (the best of the best). There is naturally some confusion about what *an* optimum really implies, and we shall return to this after laying the groundwork by discussing the component aspects in turn.

Efficiency in production

The production function bounds the range of technically feasible sets of possible values for all factors and products. Efficiency in production requires that the boundary of the feasible region be achieved, that is that it must not be possible to produce more of any product without either reducing the output of some other product or increasing the input of some factor, nor must it be possible to use less of any factor without simultaneously increasing the input of another factor, or producing less of some product. For efficiency to be achieved in this sense it is necessary that certain conditions hold for each pair of products, pair of factors and pair involving one factor and one product. For each such pair it is necessary that a

single marginal rate of transformation or marginal rate of
technical substitution hold throughout the economy.

If two firms both produce X and Y, even though they might
employ different production processes and use different
factors, and one firm could produce one additional unit of X
at the expense of producing three units less of Y, while the
other could produce four extra units of Y at the expense of
producing one less unit of X; then they could between them
produce one extra unit of Y with no loss of output of X. Their
marginal rates of transformation of X into Y would be 3 and
4 respectively; but only if these rates were equal would it be
impossible for them to increase their combined output. This
proposition is inherent in Figure 2(d) (p. 40). The slope of the
transformation curve PP′ at the point representing the aggregate outputs of X and Y for the economy as a whole is the
marginal rate of transformation for the whole economy. If
any single firm had a marginal rate of transformation between
X and Y different from this then aggregate output could be
increased if it produced more of one good and less of the other
while other firms made offsetting adjustments.

It is similarly necessary that if two firms both use factors A
and B, even though they might use them to produce different
products, then the marginal rate of technical substitution
between the two factors must be the same for both firms. If
one could substitute three units of A for one of B, while the
other could substitute one unit of B for four of A, then between
them they could reduce aggregate input of A by one unit with
no change in input of B or aggregate output. This proposition
was inherent in the derivation of Figure 2(d) from the points of
tangency between isoquants on Figure 2(a). At tangency the
two isoquants have the same slope, that slope being the
marginal rate of technical substitution between A and B in
both X and Y.

Finally it is necessary that if two firms both use factor A in
the production of X, even though they might combine it with
different sets of other factors, then both must have the same
marginal physical productivity of A in X. Otherwise aggregate
output of X could be increased, or input of A reduced, if more

A were used by the firm with the higher marginal productivity and less by the other.

The Paretian value judgement is that it would be a good thing to make one person better off if no one were simultaneously made worse off. We have defined 'products' and factors 'such that individuals would rather have more products than less and would rather provide fewer factor services than more. Clearly a Paretian improvement would be possible if efficiency in production in the above sense were not achieved. Since a Paretian optimum is a position in which no further Paretian improvement is possible, it follows that efficiency in production is necessary for the achievement of a Paretian optimum. Although necessary, efficiency in production is not sufficient for a Paretian optimum, for we might be producing the wrong goods albeit in an efficient way, or those goods might be wrongly distributed among consumers. The latter possibility leads us to an examination of efficiency in exchange.

Efficiency in exchange

Just as it is necessary for efficiency in production that all firms producing two products X and Y have the same marginal rate of transformation between them, so it is necessary for efficiency in exchange that all persons consuming both have the same marginal rate of substitution between them. Otherwise a simple act of exchange could make both parties better off without changing aggregate consumption. This principle was inherent in Figure 9 (p. 62), as it was in earlier figures. Only points of tangency between indifference curves can be efficient distributions of goods, for there the curves have the same slope and that slope represents the marginal rate of substitution. Where indifference curves of the two parties intersect they have different slopes, the marginal rates of substitution differ, and a simple act of exchange would make both better off.

It is similarly necessary that, if two persons both provide factor services A and B, their marginal rates of substitution between them be equal. Otherwise both could be better off if one provided more A and less B and the other the converse. This principle was inherent in the tangency between indifference curves in Figure 10 (p. 63). Finally it is necessary that two persons both providing A and consuming X have the same marginal rate of substitution between them. Otherwise they would both be better off if one provided more A and consumed more X while the other provided and consumed less. This principle underlay the tangency of indifference curves in Figure 11 (p. 64).

Efficiency in both production and exchange

The necessary conditions for efficiency in production and exchange require, respectively, that the bundle of factors used and goods produced in the economy be so organized that greater output is impossible without greater cost, and that the bundle be so distributed that greater satisfaction for one person is impossible without less for another. Independently, however, they do not ensure that the right bundle of goods and factors is chosen. For this it is necessary that the common marginal rate of transformation between any two goods be equal to the common marginal rate of substitution. Otherwise it would be possible to make all persons better off by producing more of one good and less of another. Similarly the marginal rate of technical substitution between any two factors must be equal to the marginal rate of indifferent substitution and the marginal productivity of a factor in the production of a good must equal the marginal rate of indifferent substitution between them.

These propositions are illustrated by Figures 9, 10, and 11 respectively. In each case the utility possibility curve U'_{I}, U'_{II} is tangent to the constraint at the optimum point. The slope of the former is the common marginal rate of indifferent substitution and that of the latter the common marginal rate of transformation.

Paretian optima and the optimum optimorum

Satisfaction of the conditions of efficiency in production and exchange is necessary for the achievement of an optimum in a Paretian world, for if any of the conditions were violated then it would be possible to make adjustments that would result in some person being better off and no one simultaneously worse off. Fulfilment of these conditions is sufficient for the achievement of a Paretian optimum as this term is generally used in the literature, but this does not imply that a particular economic situation that satisfies the conditions is the best attainable from a welfare standpoint, nor that it is necessarily better than some other position that fails to satisfy the efficiency conditions. This apparent contradiction is readily resolved when we view the conditions of efficiency in both commodity and utility space.

All the conditions that we have so far discussed have been postulated in commodity or factor terms. They were all encompassed in the translation of the transformation function, through the medium of utility functions, from commodity into utility space to derive the utility frontier. All these conditions will be simultaneously satisfied at all points on the utility possibility frontier. But that frontier represents the constraint in utility space, not the objective. The Paretian value judgement requires that welfare be a positive function of utility levels, and optimization therefore requires that we be on the frontier in utility space. Fulfilment of the efficiency conditions is necessary to the achievement of the optimum optimorum. But it is not sufficient, for those conditions are fulfilled at all points on the frontier, but at only one point is that frontier tangent to a contour of the welfare function. It is the satisfaction of this tangency condition that distinguishes the optimum optimorum from other 'Paretian optima'. This requires efficiency in distribution in the sense that it is not possible to make one person better off, at the expense of making someone else worse off, in such manner as to increase the level of welfare. Formally, the marginal rate of possible substitution between the utility levels of any two individuals must equal the marginal rate of welfare indifferent substitution.

Figure 14 illustrates these propositions in utility space. UU is the utility possibility frontier derived from the transformation function via the utility functions. Points A, B, C, D and E are all points on the frontier, all are Paretian optima and all the efficiency conditions of production and exchange are satisfied at all of them. Some of those conditions are violated at F, however, for F although within the feasible area is not on the frontier. Three contours of a welfare function are shown and the optimum optimorum is at the tangency point C. Point F could not be an optimum optimorum for there must be points

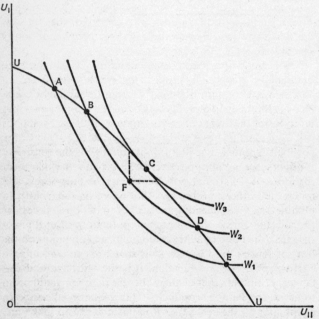

Figure 14

on the frontier north-east of F that yield greater welfare. Being on the frontier is a necessary condition for maximum welfare, and all the efficiency conditions of production and exchange are necessary to being on the frontier. But they are not sufficient for the maximization of welfare, for they are all satisfied at A and E, yet point F which violates some of them yields greater welfare than either A or E. A movement from F to A, which would involve satisfying some of the efficiency conditions that were previously violated, and violating none, would actually reduce the level of welfare if the value judgements about distribution were such as to yield the welfare function shown. Mere satisfaction of efficiency conditions previously violated does not ensure an increase in welfare unless we combine it with knowledge of the welfare function. Movement from F to a position north-east of F would ensure an increase in welfare, but we could know that a new situation postulated in commodity terms would lie north-east of F in utility space only if we knew the properties of utility functions.

The concept of *a* Paretian optimum and of the efficiency conditions of production and exchange are thus seen to be very treacherous as a guide to policy. Without knowledge of either utility functions or the welfare function we cannot be sure that satisfying those conditions is better than violating them.

Sufficient conditions for optimality

We have so far been concerned with the first-order, or marginal, conditions of the optimum. These may be summarized by saying that whenever it is possible to change the values of two variables, without affecting the values of others, the rate of possible substitution must be common throughout the economy, the rate of indifferent substitution must be common and the rates of possible and indifferent substitution must be equal. This statement holds whether the variables are commodities, factors or one commodity and one factor. It is a necessary condition for the achievement of a Paretian optimum. For the optimum optimorum it is further necessary that the same statement hold with respect to two utility levels as the variables, in which case indifferent substitution refers to welfare indifference rather than utility indifference.

The same condition is necessary for a dynamic optimum by interpreting the two variables as having reference to the same factor or good at different moments in time. If individuals were just willing to sacrifice 100 units of a commodity today, in exchange for 105 units of the same commodity one year hence, the marginal rate of substitution would be 1·05 and the marginal rate of time preference 5 per cent per annum. If different persons had different marginal rates of time preference a simple act of exchange could make both better off, the form of exchange in this case being a loan at a positive rate of interest. If it were technically possible to reduce output today by 100 units, divert resources to investment and thereby increase output one year hence by 105 units, then the marginal rate of transformation would be $1 \cdot 05$ and the marginal efficiency of capital 5 per cent. If the marginal efficiency of capital exceeded the marginal rate of time preference, then all persons could be made better off by devoting more resources to saving and investment and less to current consumption, and vice versa if the rate of time preference exceeded the marginal efficiency of capital. In this way the marginal conditions provide a criterion of the optimum rate of growth as well as of the optimum utilization and allocation of resources. There are, however, difficulties if a long time span is considered, for the individuals alive at the end of the period are not the same people as those alive at the beginning. The problem of deciding to what extent we should enjoy greater affluence today, and to what extent we should instead build a more productive world for our children, is inherent in questions of optimal rates of growth, resource conservation, etc. The theoretical solution would involve not only distributional value judgements between this generation and future ones, but also assumptions about the nature of the utility functions of future generations. The relevant value judgements would also depend on the anticipated social conscience of future generations as well as our own. Welfare economics offers no ready means by which the relevant information can be acquired, but it does enable us to pinpoint the fundamental issues involved in some of the crucial areas about which our society must somehow make decisions through the political process.

Satisfaction of the marginal, or first-order, conditions, while necessary for the maximization of welfare is not sufficient, for they might define a minimum rather than a maximum solution. To ensure that we have a maximum it is necessary that appropriate second-order conditions are also satisfied. In the calculus these conditions are satisfied if the second-order derivatives have appropriate sign. In the geometry they will be satisfied if the functions are convex, and the assumptions that ensure convexity were examined in previous chapters. Together the first- and second-order conditions ensure a local maximum. If the functions are everywhere convex we have a global maximum, but if there are alternating convexities and concavities in the functions there will be multiple local maxima and the first- and second-order conditions do not enable us to distinguish the maximum maximorum. If we think of all possible economic situations as being represented by points on a plane and the welfare associated with each situation by a perpendicular distance from the plane, then local concavities in the functions would result in a surface resembling a range of hills. The first-order, or marginal, conditions distinguish all points where the surface is horizontal, including the tops of hills and the bottoms of valleys. From this set the second-order, or convexity, conditions identify the hilltops, but do not tell us which is the highest hilltop. If there are no concavities, however, there is only one hill and its top is the highest point.

Finally we must consider the possibility of corner solutions. The first and second-order conditions together refer only to factors and goods of which positive volumes are employed and produced. They do not ensure that welfare could not be increased if we produced a possible good of which none is currently produced. Zero volumes for some variables can be encompassed in the marginal conditions by restating the first order conditions as inequalities. Let Y be a good of which a positive volume is produced, while X is a good of which either none or some is produced. The marginal rate of transformation of X for Y is the amount of Y that would have to be sacrificed to produce one more unit of X, all other volumes of goods and factors unchanged. The marginal rate of substitution of X for Y is the greatest amount of Y that any person would sacrifice to acquire one (more) unit of X. Optimality then requires that the $MRT_{XY} \geqslant MRS_{XY}$. If this condition is satisfied it would not be worth producing another unit of X. If it holds in all cases where the second subscript represents a good of which some is produced, then it replaces the simple equality, whether or not the output of the good represented by the first subscript is positive. If both goods are produced then it would be necessary that $MRT_{XY} \geqslant MRS_{XY}$ and $MRT_{YX} \geqslant MRS_{YX}$, which could be true only if both were equalities. Definition of the MRS_{XY} as that of the person willing to sacrifice most Y to acquire one X is relevant where no X is produced, for it is not then necessary that all consumers have the same MRS, since no exchange is possible if there is no X to trade. If both X and Y are produced so that the inequality must hold in both directions, then inequality in MRS is ruled out automatically.

If $MRS_{XYI} \geqslant MRS_{XYII}$, then
$$MRS_{YXI} = \frac{1}{MRS_{XYI}} \leqslant \frac{1}{MRS_{XYII}} = MRS_{YXII}.$$

If both X and Y are produced it is required that

$$MRT_{XY} \geqslant MRS_{YXI} \geqslant MRS_{XYII} \qquad\qquad 1$$

and $\quad MRT_{YX} = \dfrac{1}{MRT_{XY}} \geqslant \dfrac{1}{MRS_{XYII}} \geqslant \dfrac{1}{MRS_{XYI}}. \qquad 2$

But **2** implies
$$MRT_{XY} \leqslant MRS_{XYII} \leqslant MRS_{XYI}. \qquad\qquad\qquad \textbf{2a}$$

Combining **1** and **2a** we have
$$MRT_{XY} \geqslant MRS_{XYI} \geqslant MRS_{XYII} \geqslant MRT_{XY}.$$

This can hold only if
$$MRT_{XY} = MRS_{XYI} = MRS_{XYII}.$$

The marginal conditions can be amended similarly to encompass the possibility of zero use of a factor. While the expressions involving inequalities are more general than those with equalities, for they encompass zero as well as positive volumes of factors and goods, they are more cumbersome to work with and we shall henceforth use the equalities for simplicity. Where the possibility of corner solutions is important it could always be included by restatement in inequalities and our simplification will not therefore affect the generality of our conclusions. *(which are not anyway !)*

Part Two
Corollaries of the Paretian Optimum

5 The Optimality of Perfect Competition

In Part One we discussed, in a theoretical context, the necessary conditions for optimality in a simple model in which only private goods existed, utility functions were independent and all functions were convex. In this chapter we shall examine how far the equilibrium state of a perfectly competitive market system will achieve the conditions of optimality. We shall then be in a position to examine the consequences of unavoidable imperfections of the market system and of interdependencies among production functions and utility functions.

The assumptions made in Part One are retained in this chapter. We shall continue to assume that all goods are purely private and that there are no externalities, that utility functions are independent and that all functions are convex. Convexity of production functions rules out the case of decreasing costs that give rise to natural monopoly. It also ensures diminishing returns. In addition we now introduce the set of behavioural assumptions that constitute the model of perfect competition. All factors and products are privately owned and individuals are free to exchange and to produce. All individuals behave as though they could not influence prices, exchanging at prevailing market price ratios and producing subject to known production functions in such manner as to maximize utility. Prices adjust automatically in accordance with the laws of supply and demand, the price of any good rising relative to other prices if there is a shortage and falling if there is a surplus. The question is whether the general equilibrium resulting from such behaviour satisfies the necessary conditions for optimality.

The analysis of the perfectly competitive system is available in any good textbook of microeconomic theory. We shall assume familiarity with it. The conclusions of such analysis stipulate the properties of equilibrium, but it is essential to remember that equilibrium is a concept quite distinct from optimum. The equilibrium position is simply the set of values for all variables that will be achieved when all forces in the model have worked themselves out, whether or not the resulting economic situation is in any sense desirable. The optimum stipulates the desirable situation whether or not it will be achieved. Positive economic theory defines the equilibrium, the analysis of Part One defined the Paretian optimum. We must now examine whether they coincide.

Let us first consider the conventional model of the profit-maximizing firm, in which the factors owned by the entrepreneur are either regarded as a fixed input, or are variable in quantity, the entrepreneur being indifferent about the extent of their use at an implicit return equal to their market price. Each entrepreneur adjusts his volumes of factors and products, subject to the production function, in the light of prevailing prices so as to maximize profit.

At the profit-maximizing position the marginal rate of transformation between any two products must be equated to the prevailing price ratio between them, for otherwise total revenue could be increased, with no change in costs, by producing more of one and less of the other. Since all producers are governed by the same price ratios, which they are powerless to influence, there will exist a common marginal rate of transformation throughout the economy for each pair of products. The same price ratios will govern consumers, and utility-maximizing behaviour requires that each consumer equate his marginal rate of substitution between any pair of products to the prevailing price ratio. The existence of an equilibrium set of prices, beyond the control of either producer or consumer, thus ensures that a uniform marginal rate of transformation between each pair of products exists throughout the economy and that this is equal to the uniform marginal rate of substitution.

Each firm must similarly equate the marginal rate of technical substitution between any pair of factors to the prevailing price ratio between them, for otherwise total costs could be reduced with no change in total revenue by using more of one and less of the other. Similarly each household will equate the marginal rate of indifferent substitution between each pair of factors to the prevailing price ratio in order to maximize utility. Again the existence of an equilibrium set of prices ensures that a common marginal rate of technical substitution for each pair of factors exists throughout the economy, and that this is equal to the common marginal rate of indifferent substitution.

In the same way the existence of an equilibrium price ratio between each pair of one factor and one product results in each producer equating the marginal productivity of that factor in the production of that product to the prevailing price ratio, while each household equates its marginal rate of indifferent substitution between factor and product to the same price ratio.[1] Thus there exists in equilibrium a common marginal product equal to the common marginal rate of substitution.

Convexity of all production functions and utility functions ensures that the second-order conditions are satisfied, so that the necessary conditions for a static Paretian optimum are satisfied by the perfectly competitive equilibrium. If the capital market is also perfectly competitive, in the sense that there exists a standard rate of interest at which anyone may lend or borrow, that rate adjusting to an equilibrium that equates the supply of and demand for loanable funds, then each producer will equate the marginal efficiency of capital to the prevailing rate, while each household equates its marginal rate of time preference to the same rate, so that the condition for a dynamic optimum is also satisfied.

The conclusions concerning the optimality of the perfectly competitive equilibrium are not materially affected if we substitute a more general behavioural assumption of utility maximization by the entrepreneur for the conventional assumption of profit maximization. This can be done by re-defining the normal rate of profit so as to make maximization of pure profit fully compatible with utility maximization.

1. It is assumed that factors are divisible, that workers are free to vary their hours of work at prevailing wage rates.

Total revenue of the firm and total explicit cost of factors purchased by the firm are readily defined, the difference between them being accounting net profit. From net profit we must deduct the implicit cost of using factors owned by the entrepreneur to leave pure profit. The implicit costs represent the normal rate of profit. There is no problem if the factors owned by the entrepreneur are fixed inputs for the implicit cost will then be a component of fixed cost, but not of marginal cost. Maximization of pure profit and of utility will coincide. If the entrepreneur attaches zero utility significance to variations in the use of factors that he owns, the marginal component of implicit cost will again be zero. Where the utilization of factors owned by the entrepreneur is variable, however, and additional use occasions disutility, their valuation is more difficult.

The cost of using each additional unit of a factor is the minimum amount that would just persuade the entrepreneur to make the sacrifice. Where homogeneous units of the same factors are owned by others and a competitive market exists in them, the market price is a measure of implicit cost. Since the entrepreneur could sell his own factors to others at the market price, that price will measure the sacrifice made as a result of using them in the firm. If the market price is too low to persuade the entrepreneur to use his factor at all, then he will purchase units from others and market price will measure the explicit cost. Where the factor is not homogeneous, however, there is no ready measure of market price. The entrepreneur may have specialized knowledge of his own business. Four different values may then attach to a marginal hour of managerial time. First is the wage rate the entrepreneur could earn selling his time to some other business, or the demand price for his time in the market (P_D). Second is the wage rate he would have to pay to hire someone equally efficient as himself at managing his own business, or the supply price of equivalent labour (P_S). Third is the value he places on his time if it remains free for leisure, or the reservation price (P_R). Fourth is the extra amount an hour of managerial time could earn in his business, or its value of marginal product (VMP). The opportunity cost to the entrepreneur of using consecutive hours of his own time in his own business is the greater of P_R or P_D, for the time could have yielded a value P_R in leisure or P_D if sold.

Now at the equilibrium position it is necessary that

$$P_S \geqslant \text{VMP} = P_R \geqslant P_D.$$

If $\text{VMP}>P_S$ then it would be profitable to hire additional managerial time in the market. If $\text{VMP} \neq P_R$, then the entrepreneur would be better off working more or fewer hours at the managerial function, depending on the direction of the inequality. If $P_D>P_R$ he would work additional hours for another employer for wages until P_R rose to the level P_D. If $P_S = P_D$, that is if there is a perfect market in homogeneous managerial time, then that price measures the implicit cost. If $P_R<P_D$ for infra-marginal hours the entrepreneur's economic rent *qua* manager will be a component of implicit cost. If no perfect market exists, however, and $P_R>P_D$ for the last few hours, the equation of VMP to P_R will imply satisfaction of the Paretian conditions. The marginal physical product of managerial time will be equated to the ratio of the price of the product to the reserve price of entrepreneurial labour. If the entrepreneur's labour is not sold to any other employer and no one else is employed by the entrepreneur to perform the managerial function, optimal corner solutions will arise with respect to other persons.

With implicit cost defined as the higher of P_D or P_R for consecutive units of factor services owned by the entrepreneur and used by the firm, pure profit represents a net surplus to the entrepreneur. Since he is already fully compensated by the normal rate of profit for the utility significance of the use of his factors, the maximization of utility coincides with the maximization of pure profit.

Valuation of implicit costs in this way, although compatible with the behavioural assumption of utility maximization by the entrepreneur, would introduce considerable complexity into the positive economic analysis of the firm. Reservation price may well be subject to an income effect. If product price rises, so that the entrepreneur would be better off with the same output, his higher income might result in his placing a higher reservation price on his factors. The cost curves would then rise, and might even rise far enough to result in equilibrium output falling in response to a rise in product price. The complexity that would arise in the geometric analysis of the firm, if the level of the cost curves varied with product price, fortunately need not concern us in the present context.

Thus we see that satisfaction of all the conditions of equilibrium in a model of perfect competition ensures that all the Paretian conditions of the production optimum and the exchange optimum will be simultaneously satisfied. Perfect competition is sufficient for the achievement of a Paretian optimum. Demonstration of this proposition tempts one to jump to the conclusion that perfect competition is the only ideal system of economic organization. Such a claim is far from warranted, however, as is apparent when we examine the relations between competition and optimality more closely.

While perfect competition is sufficient for the achievement of a Paretian optimum, it is not necessary. It is quite possible, theoretically, to satisfy the necessary conditions in a controlled socialist state. 'Perfect' socialism is every bit as good as perfect competition when judged by this criterion. In the real world, of course, Socialism is far from perfect, but so is competition. Since both systems are capable of achieving a Paretian optimum in their conceptually perfect forms, the proposition concerning perfect competition does not establish its superiority. Still less does it establish anything concerning a real world situation of imperfect competition. Perfect competition is sufficient, but not necessary, for a Paretian optimum.

As we saw in the previous chapter, the production and exchange conditions of a Paretian optimum, while necessary for the achievement of a welfare optimum (the optimum optimorum), are not sufficient. A Paretian optimum necessarily exists on the frontier in utility space, but only one point on that frontier is a welfare optimum. Which point is the welfare optimum will depend upon the value judgements in the welfare function, while the competitive equilibrium will depend on the initial distribution of factor ownership. Only by coincidence would these coincide.

Thus while perfect competition is sufficient, but not necessary, for achievement of the frontier, being on the frontier is necessary, but not sufficient, for a welfare optimum. Perfect competition is not therefore established as either necessary or sufficient for achievement of the welfare optimum.[1]

Distribution and the optimality of perfect competition

It is sometimes contended that perfect competition will achieve a welfare optimum if the initial distribution of factor endowments is considered equitable. This condition is subject to two interpretations that are rarely distinguished. It could mean that the initial distribution of factors is such that the distribution of utilities resulting from competitive equilibrium is considered equitable. This interpretation amounts to no more than a truism; if the position of the frontier achieved by perfect competition is considered optimal, it is a welfare optimum. It does, however, expose the coincidental nature of the welfare optimality of perfect competition, for the utility levels resulting from an initial factor endowment will depend on both the transformation function and the entire set of utility functions. If two persons have different initial factor endowments their relative incomes will depend on the marginal productivities of those factors, which will in turn depend on production functions and the composition of output. The latter is dependent on the demand functions that reflect the entire set of utility

1. A chain is only as strong as its weakest link, and this is true of chains of logical connection. If A is sufficient for B, but B is not sufficient for C, then A is not established as sufficient for C; if A is not necessary for B, although B is necessary for C, then A is not established as necessary for C. A might in fact be both necessary and sufficient for C but the premises do not establish that conclusion (e.g. congruency of two triangles is sufficient but not necessary for similarity, similarity is necessary but not sufficient for them to have equal sides). Or A and C might be compatible though not coincident (e.g. being a politician is sufficient but not necessary for being human, being human is necessary but not sufficient for being a conservative). Or they might be incompatible (e.g. being a man is sufficient but not necessary for being human, being human is necessary but not sufficient for being a woman). A chain containing one negative relation tells us nothing about the connections between the ends.

functions as well as on the supply functions that reflect production functions. If the initial factor endowment and the welfare function in utility space are postulated independent of the transformation function and utility functions, equilibrium will coincide with a welfare optimum only by coincidence.

The second interpretation is that the concept of equity refers not to the resulting distribution of utilities, but to the initial factor endowments themselves. The stipulation of distributional value judgements in terms of initial factor ownership is fully compatible with the concept of property rights and the philosophy of *laissez-faire*, but it is incompatible with the welfare function in utility space that we have previously assumed. It is a formulation of the welfare function that is interesting both from the theoretical and the historical points of view and deserves closer consideration.

The philosophical premise that the individual is entitled to freedom of the person and the fruits of his own labour is a value judgement defining equitable distribution of the factor labour. Distribution of the ownership of land and capital (collectively referred to as property rights) is sanctioned by concepts of private property, inheritance and freedom to accumulate. That some families are rich and some poor might be attributed to historical accident or divine providence,[1] provided that the particular distribution is accepted as right and proper. Such a set of value judgements would suffice in a non-exchange economy with traditional technology, for the relationship between distributions of factor ownership and real income could persist virtually unchanged through time, so that the question whether equity referred to the former or the latter would not arise. Only relative holdings of capital would change if different families had different propensities to save, and if such changes were viewed as the ethically proper consequences of thrift and profligacy, they would be accepted as desirable.

Development of the exchange economy gave rise to the philo-

1. A popular hymn of the Church of England included until recently the lines, 'The rich man in his castle, the poor man at his gate, He made them high or lowly, and ordered their estate'.

sophical question of the just price, for prices were properly recognized as the linkage between the distribution of factors and the distribution of products. Adam Smith's concept of the invisible hand, and the subsequent demonstration of the efficiency of the perfectly competitive general equilibrium, reconciled the equilibrium price with the just price (see Worland, 1967). A teleological interpretation of economic activity leads to the conclusion that the distribution of products should follow from the distribution of factor ownership. If the latter is accepted as ordained by higher authority, while marginal products reflect the state of nature, the resulting distribution of goods is automatically accepted. If the role of government is limited to the maintenance of law and order, i.e. the protection of vested property rights, and such other functions as may be sanctioned by the divine right of kings, the value judgement problems of welfare economics do not arise. The analytical device of postulating a welfare function dictated by some *deus ex machina* simply formalizes the concept of natural law on which the defence of the distributive justice of the competitive system ultimately rests. It is only when the power to make value judgements is claimed as a human right to be exercised through some process of constitutional government that problems arise. For not only is there then no superior source of ethics to which to appeal, but the automatic coincidence of equitable distributions of factors, products and utility no longer holds. We are not only forced to decide what value judgements to make, but what to make value judgements about.

The perfectly competitive system is dependent on private ownership of factors of production, but the acceptance of an initial distribution of factors, independent of the transformation function, precludes our having value judgements about the distribution of utilities. We cannot judge a perfectly competitive system by the equity of the outcome, for the essence of the system is that distributive justice is an attribute of the inputs of the system, not the outputs. In a stationary state there is no problem, for the relationship between the distributions of factors and real income is constant. Nor is there a problem if changing technology or market conditions are interpreted as governed by the laws of nature or by divine providence, for any impact on the distribution of real income is then presumed to be equitable by natural law or higher authority. But such a system cannot offer guidance on the policies to be pursued by a secular government when these will affect the distribution of utilities.

Consider, for example, the case of a closed economy producing two goods X and Y from factors A and B in perfectly competitive static equilibrium. Product X is A intensive and Y is B intensive. The possibility now arises of opening this economy to free world trade. The country in question would have a comparative advantage in X so that the effect of trade would be to raise the P_X/P_Y ratio, making the owners of factor A better off and those of B worse off. Whether free trade would be a good thing cannot depend on distributional value judgements if these are made exclusively about factor ownership, for the ownership of factors would not be affected. Suppose it would be true that a redistribution of income from the owners of A to those of B, together with free trade, could make everyone better off.[1] We could then say that free trade with compensation would be better than no trade on Paretian grounds. But to ask whether free trade with redistribution would be better than trade without is to suggest that distributional value judgements should be made in utility space. Without them we could not decide whether redistribution would be desirable, and without an answer to that question we could not decide whether free trade, without compensation, would be a good thing.[2] Free trade would achieve a point on the Paretian boundary, while prohibition of trade would not. But to express concern over the distributional consequences and to consider redistribution of income to offset them, would be to deny that the owners of factor A are entitled to the full proceeds of their productivity in an open competitive system. This undermines the concept of property rights on which the competitive system is based.

A system in which distributional equity is thought of in

1. This is the compensation principle. See chapter 8.
2. This case, although simplified, illustrates the essential feature of the famous debate over repeal of the Corn Laws.

terms of utilities or incomes, but which also subscribes to the principles of private property and free exchange, can be rationalized by a welfare function in utility space, the weights attaching to individual utilities being governed in part by the ownership of factors. The consequence of a welfare function in this form would be the judgement that an individual is entitled to a certain income (or share of total income) because he owns certain factors. This accords with the concept of a 'fair' price for a factor that differs from the competitive equilibrium price. The result is two sets of prices, one based on market forces on which the allocative optimality of perfect competition depends, and one based on value judgements and designed to achieve an equitable distribution of income among factor owners. The dilemma occasioned by such dual-pricing criteria underlies much of the difficulty encountered with agricultural price-support programmes. If such attempts are made to superimpose equity on the competitive equilibrium then its efficiency is jeopardized. If income transfers are achieved by progressive taxation, then the marginal conditions of optimality that follow from the motivational assumption of the competitive model are violated. If the distribution of factor ownership is adjusted to maintain equitable income distribution then the concept of private property is violated. The rights to factors are then vested in the government and their association with individuals is a temporary matter of convenience.

Thus either the competitive equilibrium achieves distributional equity as a matter of definition, because equity existed in the initial pattern of factor ownership, and therefore exists in the results that ensue therefrom; or equity is considered to be an attribute of the distribution of income or utility, rather than factor ownership, in which case any effort to achieve distributional equity in a changing world undermines the foundations on which the efficiency of the competitive system was based. Either the welfare function is in factor space, and perfect competition necessarily achieves both efficiency and equity, for the equity is built into the premises; or the welfare function is in utility (or income) space, in which case perfect competition and equity are in general incompatible.

6 Optimization in an Imperfect World

In the preceding chapter we examined how far an economy of perfect competition would, in equilibrium, achieve the conditions of optimality. While a useful abstraction for analytical purposes, the model of perfect competition differs in many of its assumptions from the facts of the real world. In this chapter we shall consider how the conclusions derived from the analysis of perfect competition can be extended to encompass some of the important cases in the real world that violate the assumptions of the perfectly competitive norm.

We have so far been concerned with perfectly competitive firms, paying little attention to industries. As is well known industries can exhibit increasing, decreasing or constant costs. While the case of constant-cost industries gives rise to no problems, much attention has been focused in the literature on the question whether increasing- and decreasing-cost industries achieve fulfilment of the Paretian conditions even in a world of perfect competition. This question deserves brief examination before we relax the assumptions of perfect competition.

Increasing- and decreasing-cost industries

An increasing-cost industry is one in which the average cost of production rises as the output of the industry rises. Marginal cost of the industry is therefore above average cost. Since, in equilibrium, industry average cost equals both average and marginal cost of the firm, and these are equated to price, it follows that industry marginal cost exceeds price. It might therefore be suspected that increasing-cost industries produce more than optimum output, and it has been proposed that such industries should be taxed so as to equate price and industry marginal cost.

Increasing costs might exist for two distinct reasons. The simplest case occurs because the supply curves of factors used in the industry are themselves upward sloping. Although each single firm is such a small buyer of those factors that it alone can have no significant influence on their prices, simultaneous expansion of all firms in an industry might so increase the demand for factors that their prices, and accordingly the costs of all firms, might rise significantly.

The higher level of average cost is attributable to the higher factor prices that must be paid to attract additional volumes of factors to the industry. These higher factor prices must be paid for all units of the factor, not only the additional units, and average cost for infra-marginal units of the product rises because the marginal unit is produced. This additional cost on infra-marginal units constitutes the excess of industry marginal cost over industry average cost. The buyer of the marginal unit of product considers it only just worth its price, and that price only just covers the average cost of production. The additional costs of infra-marginal units are not included in the price paid by the marginal buyer and it has therefore been argued that in social terms the last unit was not worth its cost. By extension of this argument the conclusion is reached that optimum output requires equation of price and industry marginal cost, and that this could be achieved by a tax that forced the buyer of the marginal unit to pay for the additional costs incurred for infra-marginal units.

In order to expose the fallacy in this argument we must examine carefully what is meant by 'cost'. The real cost of infra-marginal units, measured in units of factors absorbed in their production, has not changed; but the money cost has increased because factor prices have risen. Buyers of infra-marginal units of product are accordingly forced to pay more, while owners of infra-marginal units of factors receive more. Certainly there is a loss of consumers' surplus, but this is precisely offset by a gain in factor rent. The effect is purely a transfer item from consumers to factor owners, a matter of possible distributional interest, but not an item of real cost of concern in allocation terms.

The second case arises where one of the factors of production is not privately owned and is treated as a free good even though it is scarce. The cost of catching sea fish, measured in real terms of hours of boat- and crew-time per ton of fish caught, from a fishing ground of finite area will, beyond some level, rise as more boats extract more fish from the sea. If each boat constitutes a competitive firm the fishing industry might well exhibit increasing costs. This case is quite different from the previous case, for the rising costs are now due not to rising wage rates but to greater real quantities of factors being absorbed per unit of output. The sea is treated as a free factor even though it is clearly scarce as soon as costs begin to rise. Increased output of fish results in a rise in the price and infra-marginal buyers lose consumers' surplus. But this is not merely a transfer item to factor owners in the form of higher wages; it is a real increase in factor costs. There is clearly reason in this case to restrict output by some form of levy included in the price of fish, so that the total price will cover the full additional real factor cost of producing the marginal unit. If the fishing ground were privately (competitively) owned, rent would be paid for fishing rights, or royalties paid on fish caught. Rent theory shows that such rent would constitute precisely the right levy to achieve the optimum conditions, just as rising factor rents constituted a precisely effective check on over-production in the previous case discussed. In that case there was no need for a tax to prevent over-production with increasing costs, because the increasing costs were caused by rising rents and the rents were already regulating production. In the fishing case there is need for a tax, or some other form of regulation, not because rent is rising but because it is not. The case for taxation of an increasing-cost industry, as an alternate to market rent on a scarce factor, is sound, but the case for a tax because rent is being paid is not.

The fault giving rise to over-production in the fishing-ground case arises because a scarce factor is treated as though it were free. Many such cases have arisen and our society appears to be remarkably slow in learning the lesson common to all. Over-grazing of medieval common (free) pasture resulted in poor quality cattle. That lesson was learned centuries ago but today we still overcrowd our (free) roads with vehicles and over-pollute our (free) air and water. Economists should be particularly careful to remember that a free factor is one that is not scarce, not simply one for which no price is charged.

We have considered two quite different cases that can give rise to increasing costs. One case that cannot arise in a competitive system is decreasing returns to scale in the production function itself.[1] Any production process can be duplicated if homogeneous factors are available. Non-multiplicability of the production function itself is a scientific impossibility, for it implies a valid experiment that cannot be repeated. The converse case of indivisibility, however, can exist and can give rise to decreasing costs.

Decreasing-cost industries are defined as the converse of increasing-cost industries, being cases where average cost falls as output rises. The cause of decreasing costs is not the converse of the cause of increasing costs, however. While upward-sloping factor supply curves can give rise to increasing costs, backward-sloping factor supply curves cannot result in decreasing costs. If the demand curve for the factor, derived from the demand curve for the product, is more elastic than the factor supply curve, the increased product demand would result in rising not falling factor price and an increase in factor rent, although in this case total output would fall. If the factor demand curve is less elastic than the supply curve there is not a stable equilibrium. Similarly while increasing costs can arise because of over-use of a scarce factor on which rents are not charged, decreasing costs cannot arise in an analogous way.

The one case that can give rise to decreasing costs occurs

1. In a firm there can be decreasing returns if the factor enterprise is not increased in proportion with other factors. Such managerial diseconomies are a very real phenomenon when a firm grows beyond a certain size, but they cannot be caused by expansion of an industry consisting of more firms, each of optimum size.

where there are increasing returns to scale resulting from indivisibilities. If the production function for either a factor or the product exhibits this characteristic it is necessarily true that the optimum output from an optimum scale of plant (in the sense of that output at which average cost would be minimized) would be greater than that currently produced. Perfect competition could not then exist. It would be possible for an item of capital (e.g. a component part) to be produced under conditions of decreasing cost and imperfect competition while the firms using that factor to produce the final product are sufficiently numerous to constitute an industry of perfect competition. The final product might then be produced under conditions of decreasing cost, for increased output by the industry might result in reduced factor prices for all firms. Such a situation would necessarily imply that the industry producing the capital is not one of perfect competition. Thus even though a perfectly competitive industry might exhibit decreasing costs it is impossible for this phenomenon to arise in a perfectly competitive economy. The phenomenon is essentially one of imperfect competition and is the heart of the controversy surrounding the principle of marginal-cost pricing.

The marginal-cost pricing principle[1]

From the early work of Marshall and Pigou concerning increasing- and decreasing-cost industries, which had been based on the concept of consumers' surplus, there evolved the thesis that all prices should be equated to marginal cost. The later and more general statements of this proposition were based on the Paretian conditions of optimality. The essence of the principle can be stated very simply, but its ramifications and implications have produced an involved, and at times confused, literature.

The conditions of optimality require the equation of the marginal rate of substitution and the marginal rate of transformation for any two goods. Rational consumers equate the marginal rate of substitution to the price ratio while the marginal

1. An excellent survey of the literature on marginal cost pricing is contained in two articles by Nancy Ruggles (Ruggles, 1949–50 a and b).

rate of transformation emerges in a monetary system as a ratio of marginal costs. If the ratio of the prices of any two goods is equated to the ratio of their marginal costs, the marginal rate of substitution will be equated to the marginal rate of transformation. Clearly this condition will be satisfied if price is everywhere equated to marginal cost.

We have already shown that satisfaction of the marginal conditions is necessary, but not sufficient, for the achievement of a welfare optimum. The controversy surrounding the marginal-cost pricing principle can conveniently be separated into two problems; whether it is possible to satisfy the marginal conditions and whether, if possible, their satisfaction would be sufficient to support the inference that welfare would be increased.

One early version of the principle (Dickinson, 1933) advocated the establishment of a 'marginal-cost equalization fund' into which would be paid the excess of revenues over costs on increasing-cost industries and out of which would be paid the deficit on decreasing-cost industries. There is no reason to suppose that such a fund would break even, however, for it is precisely the violation of the conditions of the 'adding-up theorem'[1] that gives rise to the case for pegging prices at marginal cost. We have already shown that the case for taxing increasing-cost industries is invalid when costs increase because of rising factor rents. It is only taxes imposed in lieu of rents that would produce revenues for the fund. These would include both long-term rents on natural resources (e.g. fishing grounds) and short-term rents on capital (e.g. peak-pricing on railways). (See, for example, Hotelling, 1938.) Such sources of revenue for meeting deficits on decreasing-cost industries are only special cases of taxing rents in general, a possibility to which we shall return shortly.

In decreasing-cost industries deficits would arise because the revenues derived from prices equal to marginal costs would of

1. This theorem shows that if each factor is paid its value of marginal product and each product is priced at marginal cost then with constant returns to scale (inherent in perfect competition) factor payments will precisely exhaust the value of total output.

necessity be inadequate to meet total costs. Two separate classes of overhead costs must be considered; historic costs and continuing overheads. The historic-cost case, being purely *ex post*, is not a problem of resource allocation, though it is of distributional interest. Once a tunnel is dug it is available for use. The marginal cost of using it is independent of how much it cost to dig and it has rightly been argued that it would be foolish to discourage optimum use of the tunnel by charging prices above marginal cost in order to recoup the initial outlay. This is essentially the case for toll-free roads and bridges in the absence of congestion. Whether or not those who incurred the historic costs should be reimbursed, and if so from what sources, is a distributional question distinct from the case made on resource-allocation grounds for pricing at marginal cost. Continuing overhead costs are not as easily dismissed and give rise to the whole problem of defining the marginal unit. A simple example will illustrate this problem.

The marginal cost of carrying an additional passenger on a train that is less than full is virtually zero. If the train is full the marginal cost might include the cost of an additional carriage, or even of running an additional train. If, in the absence of congestion, passenger fares are set at a marginal cost of virtually zero, the continuing costs of running locomotives and maintaining track must be met even if we dismiss the historic cost of the tunnel as irrelevant to the allocation problem. There is no easy solution to the problem of defining the relevant unit, as is evidenced by the economist, discussing the application of marginal-cost pricing to bus fares, who suggested that the first man on the bus queue should buy the bus and the rest get on for nothing. The question how big a bus he should buy gives rise to another major problem. It is one thing to dismiss the historic cost of digging a tunnel *ex post*, but quite another to dismiss it *ex ante*. What criterion would there be under marginal-cost pricing to determine whether a proposed tunnel or other investment project is worth building at all? We shall return to this problem when we examine cost–benefit analysis.

In the literature of the marginal-cost pricing principle it has generally been assumed that, if all prices were set at marginal cost, total revenues would be inadequate to meet total costs. Various schemes of taxation and price discrimination have been proposed as possible ways to cover the deficit, for the deficit on continuing overheads is a real resource cost that must be covered somehow if marginal-cost pricing is to be possible. Taxes on any marginal transaction will upset the relevant optimum conditions, and ideal taxes must accordingly be non-marginal or lump sum. In a closed economy the simplest tax is a poll tax at a set rate for each citizen. In an open economy these become residence taxes and might encourage emigration. The strongest objection to poll taxes is their intense regressivity, and it is on distributional grounds that they are normally rejected. From an allocation standpoint a pure poll tax is impeccable.

The most commonly advocated non-marginal taxes are taxes on economic surplus, for these are essentially non-marginal, and there are as many forms of such taxes as there are varieties of surplus. The rent on land has been long recognized as an economic surplus and has been the basis of property taxation. State ownership of all land has been proposed as one way to maximize the tax revenues from this source. Licences and royalties for use of natural resources constitute another way in which the rent on land is diverted to the public purse. Capital can also yield economic rent in the short run, though it must not be assumed that all returns from the use of capital are surplus. The rent on land is quite distinct from the rent on houses. Where demand for the use of capital is subject to recurring peaks, rent emerges with capacity utilization. Higher charges for the services of public utilities at peak times constitute one way in which this rent can be collected to offset overheads.

Consumers' surplus is another form of non-marginal return that constitutes an ideal tax base, except for the difficulty of assessing it. Perfect discrimination enables all potential consumers' surplus to be appropriated by the seller. While perfect discrimination is impossible in practice, various forms of imperfect discrimination are practised in the form of multi-part pricing. Domestic rates for electricity often encompass much higher prices on the first few units, where surplus is high, and lower rates thereafter in an attempt not to discourage marginal use, since marginal cost is low. Highway services are similarly priced, the annual licence fee for a vehicle being an attempt to recoup consumers' surplus while marginal prices are charged through fuel taxes. Multi-part pricing has long been advocated as an ideal way to finance decreasing-cost industries, for where feasible it permits average price to equal average cost while at the same time marginal price equals marginal cost. In practice, of course, only approximations to this ideal are possible.

If either the demand curve or the supply curve of a commodity or factor is perfectly inelastic there is a potential source of surplus taxation, and this is the one case where marginal taxation does not affect achievement of a Paretian optimum. If the supply curve of labour is perfectly inelastic, income taxes are taxes on surplus and have no disincentive effects. Income taxation is a very attractive means of financing the deficit on decreasing-cost industries, for it can be geared to achieve almost any set of distributional value judgements. If the labour supply curve is not perfectly inelastic then income taxation has the same fault as any other marginal tax, for it would preclude equation of the marginal rate of substitution between income and leisure with the marginal productivity of labour. An income tax is an excise on a factor. Excise taxes on goods are similarly compatible with a Paretian optimum if the demand curve is perfectly inelastic. The controversy over the relative attractions of income- and commodity-taxation involves no theoretical dispute. There is factual dispute concerning the relevant elasticities of supply and demand curves, but since the typical household exchanges factor services for goods there appears no reason to suppose that product demand curves will in general be either more or less elastic than factor supply curves. The popularity of income taxation is largely attributable to the ease with which varying degrees of progressiveness can be used to implement distributional value judgements. This, of course, assumes that such judgements are made about the distribution of income.

Complete implementation of the marginal-cost pricing principle is possible in the short run if there are adequate sources of non-marginal tax revenue to cover the deficits on decreasing-cost industries. In the long run there would also have to be an appropriate investment criterion. Full adoption of the principle would achieve a Paretian optimum, but it would achieve a different Paretian optimum for each set of non-marginal taxes that might be employed. Whether any of these optima would be a welfare optimum would depend on distributional value judgements. In the absence of such judgements the adoption of marginal-cost pricing would constitute a welfare improvement from the Paretian standpoint only if taxes were so arranged that no single individual emerged worse off. It is virtually impossible to insure that no one would be worse off and without value judgements it is accordingly invalid to conclude that marginal-cost pricing would be a good thing, even though it can be shown to achieve the necessary conditions of a Pareto optimal allocation of resources.

Partial implementation of marginal-cost pricing has proven to be even more controversial than complete implementation. One form of partial implementation is advocated in the proportionality thesis. It has been argued that, since all the Paretian conditions are expressed in terms of ratios, if the ratio of price to marginal cost is everywhere uniform these conditions will be satisfied even though that ratio is greater than one. Such an argument is clearly attractive, for the ratio could be adjusted so that total revenue from the sale of all goods would equal total costs, thereby covering the deficit on decreasing-cost industries. While perfectly valid when applied only to commodities this thesis breaks down if tested against the full set of Paretian conditions. Its application to factor prices as well as product prices would be consistent only if the common ratio were one. If applied to commodities only, a ratio greater than one would be identical to marginal-cost pricing plus a uniform rate of *ad valorem* excise tax. If we overlook savings this would in turn be the same as proportional income taxation. It is not then surprising that the proportionality thesis has been shown to be valid only if factor supply curves are perfectly inelastic. To avoid double mark-ups it is also necessary to assume that no good is simultaneously an intermediate good and a final good. The proportionality thesis is but one example of a whole class of possibilities each of which encompasses satisfaction of all the Paretian conditions but one. The last one must be assumed away as is the leisure-goods condition by the assumption of inelastic factor supplies in the proportionality thesis.

Of much greater concern for practical policy is the partial implementation of marginal-cost pricing by setting some prices equal to marginal cost in an economy where others are not. It has been widely argued that public utilities should set prices at marginal cost even though industries in the private sector do not, on the ground that it is better to satisfy the optimal conditions somewhere rather than nowhere. Such 'partial-Paretianism' has been effectively refuted by second-best theory, a development of such importance in applied welfare economics that it deserves separate consideration.

The theory of second-best

The principle inherent in the theory of second-best was discovered independently in different contexts by a number of authors. The principle was generalized by Lipsey and Lancaster (1956–7), and the interested reader is referred to their work for formal proof of the propositions below. The basic principle is both simple and devastating. The marginal conditions of the Paretian optimum are not valid criteria of an increase in welfare in a context where they are not all simultaneously satisfied. If one of those conditions cannot be fulfilled somewhere in the economy then a first-best (Paretian optimum) situation cannot be achieved. The best that can be achieved is second-best, but this requires violation of the Paretian conditions in contexts where it would be possible to satisfy them. The belief that it is better to fulfil some of the optimum conditions rather that none is false, as is the belief that it is better to depart from those conditions to a uniform extent rather than to different extents. In general, while the Paretian conditions constitute a simple statement of the necessary first-order conditions of a first-best, there is no corresponding set of rules for the achievement of a second-best, or even a better, position in a world where the first-best is unattainable. Piecemeal welfare economics based on achievement of the Paretian conditions in a partial equilibrium context may well lead to recommendations that would result in a reduction in welfare when viewed in a general equilibrium context of suboptimality.

The importance of this principle in most areas of applied welfare economics is difficult to overestimate. It is not true, for example, that public utilities or nationalized industries should price at marginal cost when other industries do not. Repeal of an apparently distorting marginal tax might reduce welfare if other marginal taxes remain in force. Repeal of tariffs on certain commodities, or on all commodities from certain countries by formation of a customs union, is not supported by the case for free trade unless free trade is universal, and the case for universal free trade is not substantiated on Paretian grounds unless all countries simultaneously achieve Paretian optimum positions internally.

The formal proofs of these propositions are normally stated algebraically and are available in the literature. A simple diagrammatic illustration of the principle will suffice for our purposes. Consider the case (Lipsey and Lancaster, 1956–7, p. 22) of an economy producing three goods X, Y and Z from one variable factor in fixed aggregate supply, under conditions of constant cost. The transformation function will be linear and is depicted in Figure 15 as the triangular plane XYZ, viewed from the perpendicular to the place. Members of the community have common tastes and incomes, the welfare function therefore coinciding with the common utility function. Contours of the function will be shaped as a nest of saucers nestling in the tripod formed by the axes. A cross-section, $T'T'$, of the space for a fixed volume of Y will show, on axes X, Z, a linear cross-section of the transformation function and a set of contours of the welfare function, as shown in Figure 16. At one point, L, the constraint $T'T'$ will be tangent to a contour of the welfare function, showing the unique point on the cross-section at which $MRS_{XZ} = MRT_{XZ}$. Other cross-sections will yield other points which together form the locus YB on the plane in Figure 15. Similar cross-sections with X as the parameter will yield the locus XA along which $MRS_{YZ} = MRT_{YZ}$; and with Z as the parameter the locus ZC along which $MRS_{XY} = MRT_{XY}$. The intersection[1] of these three loci at P

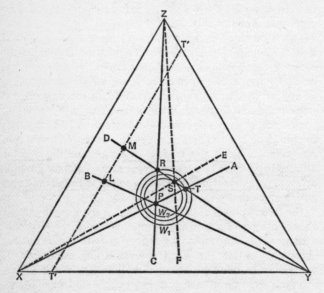

Figure 15

shows the point on the plane at which all the Paretian conditions are simultaneously satisfied. This is the first-best position at which a three-dimensional contour of the welfare function is tangent to the transformation function. It would be achieved under conditions of perfect competition.

Now suppose that industry X is operated as a monopoly charging a price above marginal cost, while Z operates under

1. If $MRS = MRT$ for two pairs of the three goods, the same condition must hold for the third pair. Thus a point at which two of the loci cross must be a point on the third.

perfect competition charging prices equal to marginal cost. Industry Y is nationalized. The problem is to determine the optimal pricing policy for Y, given the constraint that nothing can be done about pricing in either X or Z. This is a second-best situation for

$$\frac{P_X}{P_Z} > \frac{MC_X}{MC_Z}$$

and therefore $MRS_{XZ} > MRT_{XZ}$. One of the Paretian conditions is violated. Whatever price is charged for Y there will be established a set of prices yielding a budget plane different from the transformation function. Equilibrium will occur where that plane is tangent to a contour of the welfare function. The slopes of the budget plane are established by the prices, its location by the condition that equilibrium must exist on the transformation function in order to satisfy the full employment condition. The locus of achievable points can be traced on the transformation plane. Pricing policies in X and Z are fixed and determined the MRS_{XZ}, shown as the slope CC′ in Figure 16. The point on T′T′ at which this MRS occurs[1] is M. Other cross-sections yield similar points which together describe the locus YD on Figure 15. YD is the second-best constraint. Any point on it can be achieved by selecting an appropriate price for Y, but it is not possible to achieve a point on the plane that lies off YD. In particular the first-best point P is no longer attainable. If price in the nationalized industry is set equal to marginal cost the condition $MRS_{YZ} = MRT_{YZ}$ will still be satisfied, the equilibrium will still be on XA, but at point T rather than P. If the price of Y is set so that

$$\frac{P_Y}{MC_Y} = \frac{P_X}{MC_X},$$

then the condition $MRS_{XY} = MRT_{XY}$ will still be satisfied, the equilibrium will still be on ZC, but at R rather than P. Violation of the marginal condition with respect to X and Z necessarily requires violation of one other Paretian condition, but the third is still achievable. The question remains whether it is better to

1. M will be a unique point if Z is a normal good.

set the price of Y so as to violate all the Paretian conditions, or to retain satisfaction on one of them, and if so which one.

The transformation plane cuts the welfare function. One contour of the welfare function is just tangent to the transformation plane at P, higher contours are unattainable and

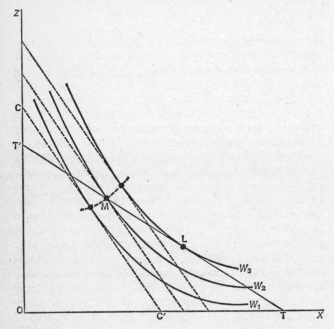

Figure 16

lower contours intersect the plane in a series of 'rings',[1] shown in Figure 15 as W_1, W_2, W_3. In this way the entire plane is ordered. It will be seen that the construction ensures that tangents to the 'rings' along XA are parallel to ZY, along YB to XZ and along ZC to XY. Whether R or T lies on the higher

1. These rings correspond to the production possibility indifference curves of McManus, from whose analysis this method had been developed. See McManus (1959).

welfare 'ring' will depend on the properties of the welfare function. Figure 15 shows the case where T lies on a higher contour than R, but it would be equally likely that this order be reversed, or that they lie on the same contour. If the utility functions are of the Cobb–Douglas type (see Lipsey and Lancaster, 1956–7, and McManus, 1959), however, it is necessary that YD diverge progressively from XY and from ZY. Since the welfare ring at T has the same slope at YZ it follows that points along YD further from Y lie on higher 'rings' than T. Similarly points closer to Y lie on higher 'rings' than R. The second-best optimum is that point on YD where it is tangent to the highest attainable welfare 'ring', at S in Figure 15. For a Cobb-Douglas welfare function it is therefore necessary that the second-best position lie between R and T.

The point S is achieved by setting the price of Y at such level that the MRS_{XY} is that depicted by the locus ZF, through S, in which case the MRS_{YZ} will automatically be that depicted by XE. The second-best constraint that requires

$$MRS_{XZ} > MRT_{XZ}$$

leads to a second-best optimum in which

$$MRS_{YZ} > MRT_{YZ} \text{ and } MRS_{XY} > MRT_{XY}.$$

All Paretian conditions are violated although one of them could have been retained. The second-best optimum price for Y is such that

$$\frac{P_X}{MC_X} > \frac{P_Y}{MC_Y} > \frac{P_Z}{MC_Z}.$$

It should be stressed that this result follows from the particular assumptions of this model. In general nothing can be said about the optimum P_Y/MC_Y ratio.

While this argument has been developed for the case of a nationalized industry, given unchangeable pricing policies of two other industries that together enforce violation of one of the Paretian conditions, the same model applies to many other cases. X could be a commodity on which an excise tax is imposed, Z a commodity on which there is no tax and Y a commodity for which it is desired to find a second-best optimal tax rate. X could represent imports subject to a tariff, Z domestic production and Y imports from a country with which a customs union is contemplated. In this case the 'transformation plane' would represent parametric terms of trade.

Conclusion

The general conclusion about optimization in an imperfect world is clear. While the first-best (necessary) conditions for a Paretian optimum are straightforward and rigorous, the corresponding conditions of a second-best optimum are complex in even the simplest model. The real world is an imperfect second-best world of far greater complexity than our simple models. In such a world there are no simple *a priori* rules for establishing a second-best optimum, nor even rigorous criteria of whether a particular change would constitute an improvement even if not an optimum. In the presence of imperfections, the best policy in any situation cannot be calculated with precision from available data. The rules of first-best optimality, coupled with the caveat of second-best, do however, constitute part of the fund of guidelines from which good, if not perfect, policy might be formulated (see, for example, Mishan, 1962). This is a delicate business, lacking scientific precision, to which we shall return in our discussion of cost–benefit analysis.

7 Joint Products, Externalities and Public Goods

In previous chapters we have limited the analysis to pure private goods and factors. It has been assumed that acts of factor supply, production, exchange and consumption are matters of total indifference to all but the immediate participants. All this is implied by the assumption of independent utility functions, that each person's utility level is governed only by his own acts of factor provision and product consumption. Further it has been assumed that all production and utility functions are continuously differentiable, which implies that the volume of any factor or product in any function can be changed, the change being offset by a change in any other variable, all others remaining constant. Only by these assumptions has it been possible to apply the marginal equivalencies of Paretian optimality on a *ceteris paribus* basis.

In the real world there are many cases where these assumptions do not hold. In this chapter we shall consider cases in which a change in the value of one variable necessarily implies a corresponding change in some other particular variable, as well as an offsetting adjustment. In such cases it is not possible to specify marginal rates of substitution, for pure substitution is not possible. Such rigid complementarities can arise in any function. If the production function requires a rigid ratio of one man one spade, it is meaningless to speak of the marginal rate of technical substitution between labour and capital in the digging of holes. If the production of one sheep necessarily implies a fixed quantity of mutton and a fixed quantity of wool, it is meaningless to speak of the marginal rate of transformation between mutton and wool. If the derivation of utility from baseball requires one bat and one ball it is meaningless to speak of the marginal rate of substitution between them. The entire range of phenomena referred to as complementarities, externalities, joint products and public goods have the common feature that somewhere one of the marginal rates is meaningless. Although related in this way the cases are quite different in that the consequences of the breakdown of different marginal rates can be quite different. Let us first consider the well known case of the joint production of mutton and wool.

Joint products

Suppose that land and labour in fixed aggregate supply can be used to grow corn or to rear sheep. Sheep provide mutton and wool in fixed proportions. There are now two separate variables in the production function (corn and sheep) but three in the utility function (corn, mutton and wool). The Paretian conditions of optimality apply to production in the usual way. The marginal rate of transformation between corn and sheep must be the same for all farms producing both and the marginal rate of technical substitution of land for labour must be the same in corn growing as in sheep rearing. Similarly the conditions of optimality in exchange still apply. There must be a common marginal rate of substitution for each pair of the three goods (corn, mutton and wool) for all consumers consuming both. The top-level optimum condition, equality between the marginal rates of substitution and transformation, cannot be expressed in the usual way, however, for there is no pair of goods for which there exists both a MRS and a MRT. Consumers are prepared to sacrifice marginal corn for marginal wool *or* marginal mutton; but marginal corn can only be transformed into marginal wool *and* marginal mutton. Optimality accordingly requires that the sum of the MRS of wool for corn and the MRS of mutton for corn equals the MRT of sheep into corn.[1] The amount of corn that consumers would just sacrifice to get one extra unit of mutton *plus* the amount they would sacrifice to get one extra unit of wool must just equal the amount of corn that would have to be sacrificed to produce the sheep that

1. Mutton and wool are measured in appropriate units so that one sheep provides one mutton and one wool.

would provide both. Where the complementarity arises in consumption rather than production analagous optimum conditions hold. The MRS of baseball sets for corn must equal the MRT of bats into corn plus the MRT of balls into corn. The amount of corn that consumers would just sacrifice for an extra baseball set must equal the amount that would have to be sacrificed for the bat *plus* the amount that would have to be sacrificed to produce the ball.

Statement of the optimum condition as Σ MRS = MRT or Σ MRT = MRS is common to all cases of joint products and public goods. The two cases are occasionally treated as though they were the same, and there is also confusion between public goods and goods necessarily produced by public enterprise. In fact important distinctions exist that depend on three criteria.

The criteria

Opportunity cost. The essential feature of a pure public good is that its enjoyment by one person in no way detracts from its availability to others. Although there is opportunity cost associated with the production of a public good, zero opportunity cost attaches to its consumption. This is a special case of joint production. In order to produce the good for one consumer it is necessary simultaneously to produce the same good for others. Private goods, by contrast, are such that consumption of a unit by one person necessarily precludes consumption of the same unit by others.

Exclusion by the producer. In most cases property rights to a product are initially vested in the producer. He has the power to permit a consumer to use the good or to prevent his doing so. Under these conditions a price can be charged for use of the good. In other cases it is not possible to exclude any potential user. In such cases it is not possible to charge a price and the market system will not work. The good or service must then be produced either by charity or public enterprise.

Exclusion by the consumer. Consumption of private goods is normally voluntary. Public goods, however, may either be such that the consumer is free to consume them or not as he chooses, or the consumer may be forced to consume them whether he likes it or not.

Of the eight possible cases defined by permutating these three criteria, four are of special interest. The first is the case of the private good, the consumption of which automatically deprives others of its use, while exclusion can be practised by both producer and consumer. Free exchange is possible and the market system can work. If two such goods are produced as joint products, competitive markets could still operate and would in equilibrium achieve the appropriate conditions of optimality. In the other three cases that we shall consider there is no opportunity cost associated with consumption and the good is accordingly public rather than private.

Public goods

If exclusion can be practised by both producer and consumer, even though no opportunity cost attaches to consumption, a market system can operate. The good is a public good, but can be produced by private enterprise. The whole field of patent and copyright law falls into this category. The knowledge of how to build a steam engine is no less available to others because someone makes use of it. The beauty of a work of art is in no way lessened for others because someone enjoys it. Similarly a bridge operating below capacity is available for others even though used by some. Although the market system can function in such cases, for the owner may refuse permission to any potential user who will not pay, it necessarily fails to satisfy the optimum conditions if a marginal price is imposed. The essence of zero opportunity cost is zero marginal cost, and the one case in which the marginal-cost pricing principle is valid on allocational grounds, even in a second-best world, is when marginal cost is zero. It may well be argued that on distributional grounds an inventor should receive reward for his invention and an artist for his creation, and on dynamic grounds that some incentive is required to ensure a continuing supply of their talents. The alternative of public support implies taxation, and marginal taxes involve their own distortions. But the fact remains that if some potential user would have derived utility from a good already in existence, at no cost to anyone, but is prevented from doing so by a marginal price, the outcome is suboptimal from a Paretian standpoint. This is the whole case for toll-free roads and bridges in the absence of congestion, not that tolls could not be charged but that it would discourage optimal use to charge them. When such goods are provided privately without a marginal price they are analysed by the theory of clubs. A golf club, for example, may be open to members who pay an annual fee without a marginal charge for each game, while being closed to non-members. It is debatable whether more utility is lost by discouraging the marginal golfer in this way or by discouraging each golfer's marginal game. Either solution may be suboptimal, but an optimal solution may be unattainable. Either solution might then constitute a second-best.[1] If there is congestion, in the sense that one user detracts from the enjoyment of the facility by others, then opportunity cost is not zero and the good is not a pure public good.

The remaining two cases are both pure public goods, opportunity cost of consumption being zero, and in neither case can exclusion be practised by the producer so that private enterprise cannot work. In one case exclusion can be practised by the consumer while in the other it cannot. Radio and television transmission is often cited as a case of a pure public good where exclusion can be practised by the consumer.[2] No matter how many persons tune receiving sets to one transmission, the signal remains as strong for others to receive; but any person who does not wish to listen can switch off. Provision of the signal is therefore either an item of positive utility to the consumer or of zero utility. It cannot be of negative utility for he need not suffer it if he dislikes it. If we

(subject to neighbours!)

1. A second-best situation arises in this case because the necessity to pay for the good somehow precludes satisfying all the Paretian conditions simultaneously. It differs from the case discussed in the previous chapter in that no particular Paretian condition is necessarily violated.
2. In the UK exclusion is practised by the producer with legal support. No person may legally receive a signal without a licence.

overlook the dubious contention that the good lacks homogeneity, the optimum volume of transmission to provide requires
fulfilment of the condition that Σ MRS for all consumers with
reference to any private *numéraire* equals MRT. A transmission is worth producing on Paretian grounds if the sum of
the amounts that all users would pay for it would cover its
cost.[1]

A similar situation exists when exclusion cannot be practised
by consumers, but the possibility then exists that some or all
consumers may suffer negative utility. Every citizen is defended
by the army, even those who sympathize with the enemy.
Every neighbouring resident is awakened by church bells,
including those heathens who would rather enjoy rest on their
day of rest. The relevant Paretian condition is again Σ MRS
= MRT, but the aggregation now includes negative as well as
positive items. If the aggregate Σ MRS is negative we have the
case of a public bad. The theory of public goods can thereby
be extended to encompass public bads such as pollution. In
this case Σ MRS is negative, but so is MRT, for the bad does
not cost resources to produce; it would cost resources to
avoid producing it. Given appropriate second-order conditions,
the optimum volume of pollution still involves the Paretian
condition Σ MRS = MRT, even though both sides of the
equation are negative.

Just as the theory of private goods can be extended to encompass joint production, so can the theory of public goods. If
one of a pair of joint products is a public good, and exclusion
cannot be practised by the producer, we have an externality.
Many classifications of external effects exist in the literature.
Some of them we have discussed,[2] but one of the most common
cases is best analysed by public goods theory.

1. The demand curve for a public good is the vertical sum of individuals' demand curves, while for a private good it is the horizontal sum.
The demand curve for a public good shows the aggregate amount that
all would pay to enjoy the same units, while the demand curve for a
private good shows the aggregate number of units consumers would
consume separately at the same price for each.

2. See chapter 6 where we discussed pecuniary externalities in the
increasing-cost case, indivisibility in the decreasing-cost case, and non-

Externalities as joint product public goods

An externality arises when an economic activity performed by
one person generates an effect, beneficial or otherwise, on some
other person who is not party to the activity.[1] Beneficial externalities are often termed external economies and harmful
ones external diseconomies. Such effects can arise either from
production or consumption. External diseconomies of production would include all forms of pollution emanating from
industrial sources, while detergent pollution from the home
would be a diseconomy of consumption. A classic case of
reciprocal external economies in production is that of neighbouring orchards and apiaries; the blossom provides the bees
with pollen to make honey, while the bees fertilize the trees.[2]
Amateur gardeners generate externalities of consumption of
both kinds; the beauty and scent of their flowers is a gift to
their neighbours while the noise of the power lawnmower is a
nuisance.

If we regard noise, smell, etc. as public goods (or bads),
externalities can readily be encompassed within the optimum
conditions. The optimum volume of such externality is such[3]
that $\Sigma \text{MRS} = \text{MRT}$. If we are concerned with an external
economy ΣMRS is positive and it is worth (from a resource
allocation standpoint) incurring additional costs to produce

payment of rent for a scarce resource in the fisheries case. In the analytical
sense it will now be recognized that the last case arose because a private
good (positive opportunity cost) was treated as though it were public.
Suboptimality arose for converse reasons in the cases discussed in this
chapter where public goods were provided privately at positive marginal
prices.

1. In this chapter we are concerned only with externalities in commodity space, that is cases in which one person is affected by another's
act of production or consumption. Externalities in utility space, i.e.
cases in which one person's utility is affected through feelings of altruism
or envy by changes in another's well-being will be considered in a later
chapter.

2. If there were no other source of pollen and no wild bees, fruit and
honey would be joint products.

3. MRS and MRT can be measured with respect to any convenient
purely private *numéraire*.

more of it, up to the point where an equivalent positive MRT occurs. If the externality is a public bad, Σ MRS is negative and it is worth incurring costs to produce less of it until an equivalent negative MRT occurs.

Many problems of the real world can be analysed in a number of ways and are challenging tests of the ingenuity of the applied-welfare economist. Congestion is an excellent example, whatever the facility congested. A municipal swimming pool, for example, can accommodate a certain number of people before they begin to inconvenience each other. Up to this number it is a public good. At some much higher level of occupancy it is impossible to get one more person in without displacing somebody else. At this stage room in the pool is a pure private good. Between these limits the service provided is neither purely public nor purely private. More persons can enter the pool, but the more that do, the lower the quality of service.[1]

If this crucial intermediate range is approached from the public goods side, then the good continues to be defined as free (uncongested) swimming, but its enjoyment by a marginal consumer simultaneously produces a local bad, congestion. Such a joint product approach to the short-run question of the optimum number of persons to permit in the pool requires that

$$\text{MRS}_i + \Sigma \text{MRS}_j = \Sigma \text{MRS} = \text{MRT}.$$

Σ MRS of the admission of a marginal swimmer will have a positive component, MRS_i, the value to him of admission to the pool, and a negative component, ΣMRS_j, the sum of the values placed by all other swimmers on the additional congestion

1. The converse of congestion arises when enjoyment of a good by some increases its utility for others. Attendance at a dance that is comfortably full may be more enjoyable than if it were poorly patronized. This relationship is rigid in games where participation of an opponent is indispensable to utility. Each consumer is then a factor of production in the provision of a service yielding utility to the other. This role is formalized where the partner is a paid professional. Such cases may be thought of as indivisibilities of consumption, but, where the relationship is not rigid, problems of defining the good result in the concept of externalities being more fruitful.

they suffer. Since no additional resources are used, MRT is zero. Alternatively we could approach the problem from the private good side and define the good as cubic feet of water per head. Admission of a marginal swimmer involves his acquiring some room from each existing swimmer and optimality requires that

$$\mathrm{MRS}_i \times V = \Sigma\, \mathrm{MRS}_j \times \frac{V}{N};$$

where i is the marginal swimmer; all $j \neq i$ the other swimmers, being N in number; and V the volume of water per head after admission of the marginal swimmer. Equality of the two marginal rates of substitution exemplifies the private aspects of room in the pool, while aggregation over j illustrates the public aspect of congestion, for all swimmers suffer the same degree of congestion. The long run question of whether to build another, or a bigger, pool can be approached in any of four ways. From either the joint public goods approach (a), or the private good approach (b), we can assume either that extra capacity accommodates additional persons with the same degree of congestion (i), or that it reduces congestion for the same number of persons (ii). These approaches yield the conditions:

(a)i $\mathrm{MRS}_i = \mathrm{MRT}$,

for each i, the relevant unit being the accommodation of one more swimmer. Since the degree of congestion is not affected

$$\Sigma\, \mathrm{MRS}_j = 0.$$

(b)i $\mathrm{MRS}_i \times V = \mathrm{MRT} \times V$,

for each i, where the relevant unit is a cubic foot of water. Dividing both sides by V makes this equivalent to (a)i.

(a)ii $-\Sigma\, \mathrm{MRS}_j = \mathrm{MRT}$,

where $-\Sigma\, \mathrm{MRS}_j$ represents the aggregate amount swimmers will pay to *reduce* congestion by accommodating one swimmer elsewhere. Since the total number of swimmers is unaffected MRS_i does not arise in this case.

(b)ii $\quad \Sigma\, MRS_j' \times \dfrac{V}{N} = MRT \times V,$

where the relevant unit is a cubic foot of water, $\Sigma\, MRS_j \times V/N$ being the aggregate amount swimmers will pay for the extra room per head afforded by accommodating one swimmer elsewhere.

The swimming-pool case is a very simple one, but exactly the same considerations are involved in many more pressing problems, including congestion of roads by traffic, and congestion of air and water by pollution. The interested student may wish to consider which approach is best suited to each of the following questions.

1. Is free admission to a congested facility ever optimal?
2. Should higher tolls be imposed on bridges during peak periods than during the off peak?
3. Should tolls on bridges be assessed per vehicle or per passenger?
4. What is the optimal degree of air pollution?
5. Should we have first-class (less congested) and economy-class swimming pools, just as we do airline seats? (~ MAS)
6. How will the optimum quantity of a facility in the long run be affected by the optimality of its use in the short run?

The modified Paretian conditions

In earlier chapters the optimum conditions for pure private goods were developed. By incorporating aggregation over relevant sets we have, in this chapter, encompassed joint products, externalities and public goods within that framework. The latter conditions are the more general, for they can encompass the entire range of possibilities from pure public goods through externalities to the opposite extreme of the pure private good. Provided that there is one purely private good in the system, which serves as *numéraire*, everything else can be considered to be a pure public good by using an appropriate definition.

While toothbrushes might be thought of as pure private goods, *my* toothbrush can be considered as a pure public good and *your* toothbrush as a different pure public good. This device of definition immediately encompasses externalities emanating from the existence of consumer goods. A fresh coat of paint on my house is of considerable value to me, of some value to my neighbours and a matter of total indifference to the residents of Timbuctoo, but it exists as a public good for all of us, even though the last group may be ignorant of its existence and would attach zero significance to it if they were informed. Externalities associated with use rather than existence can be incorporated by appropriate definition of the good. My power lawnmower might be a matter of no value to anyone while it sits in my garage, but when I produce a freshly mown lawn the local beauty, freedom from dandelion seeds and noise are generated as public goods and bads for myself, my neighbours and the residents of Timbuctoo. By such definitions the optimum conditions can be made to apply to activities as well as goods. What may normally be thought of as the externalities of my consumption of a lawnmower might become instead the externalities of the production of a mown lawn, but this is a change of no importance.

Externalities of production are incorporated by considering bundles of public goods and bads, produced as rigid complements, as vectors in commodity space. The optimum conditions can be applied as readily to a vector of goods as to a single good. Using our previous notation where X and Y are goods and A and B factors, with subscripts to identify association with persons, X_1 may be my toothbrush, X_2 your toothbrush, and Y a lighthouse. N will be a pure private good which serves as *numéraire*. We can now rewrite the optimum conditions.[1]

The conditions for efficiency in production are unaffected. It is still necessary that a common MRT, MRS or MPP exist throughout the economy for each pair of goods, pair of factors,

1. See chapter 4 for tee previous statement of the optimum conditions.

or pair of one good and one factor. The same conditions apply to any pair of vectors of production activities, each encompassing a bundle of factors and goods in fixed proportions.

The relevant condition for efficiency in production and exchange is rewritten. Instead of $MRS_{XY} = MRT_{XY}$ we have

$$\Sigma\, MRS_{x_1N} = MRT_{x_1N}$$
$$\Sigma\, MRS_{YN} = MRT_{YN}$$
$$\frac{\Sigma\, MRS_{x_1N}}{\Sigma\, MRS_{YN}} = \frac{MRT_{x_1N}}{MRT_{YN}} = MRT_{x_1Y}$$

Similar conditions apply to A, B; to A, X; to any pair involving a production vector; and to any pair involving a consumption activity. If, for example, we consider my cutting of my lawn we have the following, where a_1 is the one unit of my time spent in the activity, b_1 the one unit of fuel consumed, and x_1 the one unit of the vector of public goods and bads, beauty, noise etc., produced,

$$\frac{\Sigma\, MRS_{a_1N} + \Sigma\, MRS_{b_1N}}{\Sigma\, MRS_{x_1N}} = \frac{MRT_{a_1N} + MRT_{b_1N}}{MRT_{x_1N}}.$$

Letting V_1 be the vector of factors, one unit of a_1 plus one of b_1 being one unit of V_1, this simplifies to

$$\frac{\Sigma\, MRS_{V_1N}}{\Sigma\, MRS_{x_1N}} = \frac{MRT_{V_1N}}{MRT_{x_1N}} = MRT_{V_1x_1} = 1.$$

By expanding this we can recognize the externalities,

$$MRS^1_{a_1N} + MRS^1_{b_1N} + \sum_{i \neq 1} MRS^i_{a_1N} + \sum_{i \neq 1} MRS^i_{b_1N}$$
$$= MRS^1_{x_1N} + \sum_{i \neq 1} MRS^1_{x_1N}.$$

The first two terms on the left represent the values I place on my time and fuel and the first term on the right value I place on a mown lawn. The remaining terms are externalities, and their values may well depend on the time that the activity is undertaken. If my neighbours spend Saturday afternoons relaxing in their gardens, but Sunday mornings away from home, then $\Sigma_{i\neq 1} MRS^i_{x_1N}$ will have a lesser negative value, or higher

positive value on Sunday morning than on Saturday afternoon. If they are devout Christians who are aggrieved at the thought of my exerting myself on the sabbath while they are in church then $\Sigma_{i\neq 1} MRS^i_{a_1N}$ will have a greater value on Sunday morning

than if they are heathens relaxing on the sea shore. Unless the above equalities hold, then a <u>Paretian</u> improvement would be ? possible by my cutting my lawn more frequently, or less frequently, or at a different time.

If all the externalities are zero we have a pure private good. If $MRS^1_{xN} \neq 0$, while $MRS^i_{xN} = 0$ for each $i \neq 1$, then the good is my private good. The only effect of using the aggregate form of the condition is to add in a series of zeros that do not change the values. By comparing units of pure private goods going to different people we can derive the condition of efficiency in exchange.

$$\frac{\Sigma MRS_{x_1N}}{\Sigma MRS_{y_1N}} = \frac{MRS^1_{x_1N}+0}{MRS^1_{y_1N}+0} = \frac{MRT_{x_1N}}{MRT_{y_1N}}.$$

Thus $MRS^1_{x_1y_1} = MRT_{x_1y_1}.$
Similarly $MRS^2_{x_2y_2} = MRT_{x_2y_2}.$

The cost of producing a unit of a pure private good is the same regardless of who gets it, and therefore $MRT_{x_1y_1} = MRT_{x_2y_2}$. Accordingly $MRS^1_{x_1y_1} = MRS^2_{x_2y_2}$, which is the standard condition of a common marginal rate of substitution for all users of both goods. It is important to realize that the exchange condition is relevant only if the externalities are zero.

Conditions similar to the exchange condition apply to the geographic distribution of local public goods. If X_1, Y_1, X_2, Y_2 are units of swimming pools and bandstands in towns 1 and 2, i being the residents of 1 and j of 2, optimality requires that

$$\frac{\Sigma MRS^i_{X_1N}+\Sigma MRS^j_{X_1N}}{\Sigma MRS^i_{Y_1N}+\Sigma MRS^j_{Y_1N}} = MRT_{X_1Y_1}$$

and

$$\frac{\Sigma \, \mathrm{MRS}^i{}_{X_2N} + \Sigma \, \mathrm{MRS}^j{}_{X_2N}}{\Sigma \, \mathrm{MRS}^i{}_{Y_2N} + \Sigma \, \mathrm{MRS}^j{}_{Y_2N}} = \mathrm{MRT}_{X_2Y_2}.$$

If $\Sigma \, \mathrm{MRS}^i{}_{X_2N}$, $\Sigma \, \mathrm{MRS}^i{}_{Y_2N}$, $\Sigma \, \mathrm{MRS}^j{}_{X_1N}$, and $\Sigma \, \mathrm{MRS}^j{}_{Y_1N}$ are all zero, that is if the residents of one town have no interest in the facilities in the other, and the same MRT prevails in both places, these conditions reduce to

$$\frac{\Sigma \, \mathrm{MRS}^i{}_{X_1N}}{\Sigma \, \mathrm{MRS}^i{}_{Y_1N}} = \frac{\Sigma \, \mathrm{MRS}^j{}_{X_2N}}{\Sigma \, \mathrm{MRS}^j{}_{Y_2N}}.$$

Just as we could encompass the Paretian conditions for pure private goods in one general statement in chapter 4, so we can make a similar statement of the more general conditions from which the special case of pure private goods can be derived. Whenever it is possible to change the values of two variables, or vectors of variables, without affecting the values of others, the rate of possible substitution must be common throughout the economy and be equal to the ratio of the aggregate rates of indifferent substitution with respect to the *numéraire*.

The function of the *numéraire* in these expressions is of particular interest. It can be cancelled out in handling the MRT, but cannot be dispensed with in the MRS where aggregation is involved. It is technically possible to have a world in which only pure public goods exist, but if tastes differ it is not possible to determine a welfare-maximizing allocation unless some value judgements are made about the weight to be attached to each individual's utility function. These value judgements are subsumed in the distribution of the pure private good. To reallocate resources so as to build more swimming pools and fewer bandstands would benefit swimmers at the expense of music lovers. Neither this nor a converse change would be a Paretian improvement. If, however, private goods are simultaneously transferred from swimmers to music lovers it might be possible to leave both groups on balance better off. Optimality then requires that no such 'compensated' changes are possible. This is the basis of the compensation principle and cost–benefit analysis, which we shall examine in subsequent chapters, and is closely related to the benefit principle of taxation. The expressions $\Sigma\ \mathrm{MRS}_{XN}$ express the aggregate amount that swimmers would pay to have another pool, or the amount music lovers would accept to sacrifice a bandstand.

In an exchange economy with many private goods and a convenient medium of exchange to serve as *numéraire*, the conditions of optimality with respect to the public sector derive from the transformation function, utility functions and the chosen distribution of private goods. If all goods were purely private a perfectly competitive market system would achieve optimality through exchange and if distribution were considered equitable *laissez-faire* would be optimal. If all goods were purely public there could be no exchange. With no *numéraire* the aggregate expressions of optimality would be meaningless. Allocation would have to be determined politically and distribution would then be a question of the distribution of political power. In such a pure socialist world the question of distribution is the question of an appropriate definition of democracy.

In a mixed world where private goods are numerous, but where many public goods are produced by government, we distribute private goods through a market system modified by taxation and distribute political power through the constitution. Since both private and public goods enter utility functions there is a single Paretian optimum for any set of distributional value judgements. If, however, we have one set of values based on the concept of private property, and one based on the egalitarian distribution of voting rights, and these prevail simultaneously, there is clearly the possibility of conflict. We shall return to this fundamental dilemma in a later chapter.

Part Three
Measurement of Changes in Welfare

8 The Theory – Surplus and Compensation

The essential problem in assessing any policy decision is to determine whether welfare would be higher if some policy change is implemented than if it is not. Essentially we are concerned with the relative magnitudes of positive and negative welfare changes. In a Paretian system changes in welfare are dependent on changes in utility, and the problem therefore becomes one of assessing the impact of policy changes on individuals' utility levels, as well as that of determining the net change in welfare from a set of changes in utility levels.

One promising approach to the measurement of utility changes, which has had a chequered history in the literature of economics, is the concept of surplus. This basic concept can be applied to a number of activities, and transactions can be viewed in different directions, with the consequence that different manifestations of surplus have appeared with profusion, and some confusion. We have consumer's surplus, producer's surplus, rent, factor rent, quasi rent, economic rent and so on. These various forms of surplus arise from application of the principle in alternative partial equilibrium contexts. While the partial equilibrium applications are often the more fruitful, the basic concept is best understood in a general equilibrium setting.

Imagine a primitive economy, without exchange, in which each self-sufficient household owns its own labour and a certain amount of land from which it produces corn. The distributional value judgements of such a system are embodied in the pattern of land ownership, and the utility levels achieved constitute benchmarks from which changes can be measured. Let us now suppose that exchange develops with some convenient *numéraire*, that rent is paid for land, wages for labour and a price charged for corn. If the prevailing prices were such that some household employed its land and labour in exactly the same way as before, deriving an income that was just sufficient to purchase the amount of corn previously grown, that household would derive no surplus from exchange. Surplus could arise from a change in the terms of trade- or price-ratios. If either the rent on land or the wages of labour rose, or the price of corn fell, surplus would arise in the form of factor rent or consumer's surplus. Which it was would depend entirely on the arbitrary choice of *numéraire*, for the surplus arises not from work or consumption but from exchange at favourable price *ratios*. If money is used there is danger of double counting. Given the wage rate and rent on land, the household could pay its entire income for the amount of corn it could grow itself and derive no benefit from exchange. If the price of that amount of corn is lower the difference is consumer's surplus. If we peg rent and price, the household could work for total wages that, when added to rent received, would just buy the self-sufficient volume of corn at the prevailing price, and derive no surplus. If wage rates are higher a factor rent emerges. Thus, by pegging any two prices, surplus emerges as attributable to the third. But these are alternate ways of measuring the same surplus, they are not different components of surplus that can in any meaningful sense be added.

With the development of a complex exchange economy all households may be better off than if they were self-sufficient. The distributional value judgements embodied in property ownership that sufficed without exchange may now be relevant to only a small part of total output. The problem then arises of making and implementing relevant value judgements about the distribution of the surplus derived from exchange. The profuse literature on the 'just price', which arose with the development of the exchange economy, was concerned with precisely this problem. Attention was diverted by the development of economic theory from the question of just price to that of equilibrium price, but the former problem of what constitutes distributional equity in an exchange economy is still with us.

Use of self-sufficient output as a benchmark from which

surplus can be measured, while convenient in a simple model, is not necessary. Indeed with the development of exchange many households would be unable to maintain subsistence if self-sufficient. The utility derived from any initial set of price ratios, tax rates, legal restrictions on exchange, etc., can serve as the basis from which a change in surplus is measured, for it is with changes in the level of surplus rather than the level itself that we are concerned in assessing the impact of policy changes. The simplest cases are those in which a single price changes relative to all others. It is then most convenient to measure consumer's surplus if the price that changes is that of a consumer good, factor rent if it is a wage rate, etc., but these terms distinguish only the way in which the change in total surplus is represented; they are in no sense different forms of surplus. Consumer's surplus has been developed in greater detail than other approaches and we shall use it here, but only as an example. Any other way of looking at surplus could be used equally well and based on the same principles.

The connection between surplus and the concept of a Paretian optimum is direct. Optimality requires that it be impossible to make one person better off without simultaneously making someone else worse off, which is to say that it be impossible to effect an increase in one person's surplus without reducing that of someone else. If one person is made better off and another worse off, the question whether welfare has on balance increased requires value judgements. These similarly become necessary when surplus is aggregated over a number of individuals.

The measurement of consumer's surplus

The concept of surplus is readily depicted in classical utility theory. If we assume constant the volumes of all other goods consumed and of all factor services provided by the individual, the curve AH in Figure 17 shows the marginal utility from the consumption of X. If consumption rises from OF to OG there is an increase in utility of FBDG cardinal utils. To express surplus as a function of price rather than quantity involves further assumptions. Assume that the individual's total income and all other prices are fixed, and further assume that the marginal utility of money is constant. The individual will now maximize utility at any price of X by buying all those units for which marginal utility exceeds price multiplied by the marginal utility of money. Given the constant marginal utility of money the vertical axis can be calibrated in money rather than utils and AH is then the demand curve. If the individual were in

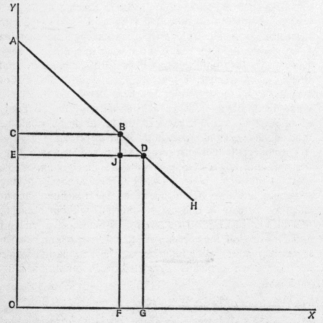

Figure 17

equilibrium at B and then received a gift of FG of X, the increase in his utility would again be FBDG, but now measured in units of money of constant marginal utility rather than in utils. If the increased quantity results not from a gift but from a fall in price from OC to OE, the surplus on the last FG units is FBDG minus the amount paid for them FJDG. In addition the individual benefits ECBJ from the price reduction on the first OF units, giving a total rise in consumer's surplus of ECBD. Unless the elasticity of demand is unitary there will be some transference of expenditure to or from other goods, but with a constant marginal utility of money this is of no consequence. By similar reasoning it is shown that the surplus on the first OF units is ABC, the area under the demand curve and above the price line.

This method of expressing consumer's surplus, and changes therein, in units of money, is based on cardinal utility and the assumption of a constant marginal utility of money.[1] These premises are unacceptable to neo-classical ordinalists and alternative measurements have accordingly been developed largely by J. R. Hicks (1956).

The top part of Figure 18 contains two contours of an individual's indifference map, with the *numéraire* (or money) measured on the vertical axis and the commodity in question, X, on the horizontal. We begin with him receiving income OM_2 and purchasing OX_1 of X at price P_2, being in equilibrium at point A on U_I. If price is reduced to P_1, he will purchase OX_4 of X, being in equilibrium at point B on U_{II}. The rise in his level of utility from U_I to U_{II} is the increase in his surplus and the problem is to express this in money. Hicks developed four different measures.

Construct a line with slope P_1 tangent to U_I (at D) to intersect the ordinate at M_1. If the individual's income is reduced by $M_1 M_2$ at the same time that price is reduced, he will be just as well off at D as he was at A. The amount $M_1 M_2$ is therefore a monetary measure of how much better off he is if price falls and there is no change in his money income. $M_1 M_2$ is called the 'compensating variation' for the price fall.

Alternatively construct a line with slope P_2 tangent to U_{II} (at C) to intersect the ordinate at M_3. If the individual's income were increased from M_2 to M_3 while price remained at P_2, he would receive the same increase in utility (at C) as the price fall alone would yield (at B). The amount $M_2 M_3$ is therefore

1. The concept originated with J. Dupuit in 1844. Marshall showed the necessity to assume a constant marginal utility of money.

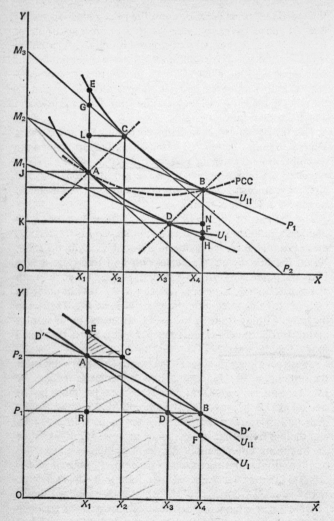

Figure 18

equivalent to the price fall and is called the 'equivalent varia-tion' for the price fall.

After the price fall he buys OX_4 at B. Following Marshall we can define the change in consumer's surplus as the amount he would be just willing to pay to acquire the additional $OX_4 - OX_1$ units, less the amount that he does pay. This concept, based on the higher quantity OX_4 rather than the lower price P_1, is measured by the distance BF, for if his income were reduced by that amount after he had achieved point B he would, at F, be neither better nor worse off than he was at A. The amount BF is called 'the compensating surplus' for the price fall.

The corresponding equivalent measurement based on the original quantity OX_1 is AE, for if that amount were added to his income at the original position, A, it would bring him to U_{II} at E. The amount AE is called the 'equivalent surplus' for the price fall.

By repeating the analysis for a rise in price from P_1 to P_2 it is readily seen that the compensating variation for the price rise equals the equivalent variation for the price fall, and the equivalent variation for the rise equals the compensating variation for the fall. Similarly the compensating surplus for the rise equals the equivalent surplus for the fall and the equivalent surplus for the rise equals the compensating surplus for the fall.

The relative sizes of these measures, and their relationship to the simple Marshallian measure previously discussed can be seen from the lower part of the diagram. The horizontal axis again measures X on the same scale as the upper part of the diagram. On the vertical axis we plot the negative of the slope of the indifference curve, or MRS_{XY}, and since in equili-brium $MRS_{XY} = P_X$, this axis also represents price. Curve ADF is therefore the negative of the first derivative of indiffer-ence curve U_I, which has $MRS = P_2$ at A and $MRS = P_1$ at D. Curve ADF is the 'compensated demand curve' derived from point A, for it shows the quantity of X demanded at each price if income is adjusted by a compensating variation so as to leave the consumer always on the indifference curve through A.

The income adjustment offsets the income effect so that the compensated demand curve shows only the substitution effect. Curve ECB is similarly derived from indifference curve U_{II}.

Area $OP_2 AX_1$ in the lower diagram is equal to JM_2 in the upper diagram, while area $X_1 ADX_3$ equals the interval KJ. By addition area $OP_2 ADX_3$ equals KM_2. The rectangular area $OP_1 DX_3$ equals KM_1 and by substraction we are left with area $P_1 P_2 AD$ equals $M_1 M_2$, as the compensating variation for the price fall. Similarly $P_1 P_2 CB$ equals $M_2 M_3$ and is the equivalent variation for the price fall.

The compensating surplus, BF in the upper diagram, equals $BH-FH$. BH, equals $M_1 M_2$, is the compensating variation and appears in the lower diagram as $P_1 P_2 AD$. $FH = NH-NF$. NH equals the area $X_3 DBX_4$ while NF equals $X_3 DFX_4$. Therefore, by subtraction, FH equals area DBF. The compensating surplus therefore, is the area $P_1 P_2 AD-DBF$, in the lower diagram. Similarly the equivalent surplus in the upper diagram is AE which equals $AG+(LE-LG)$. These intervals appear in the lower diagram as

$$P_1 P_2 CB + (X_1 ECX_2 - X_1 ACX_2)$$

and the equivalent variation is therefore $P_1 P_2 CB + AEC$.

The uncompensated demand curve AB in the lower diagram is derived from the price consumption curve in the usual way. This involves plotting for each quantity of X the slope of the indifference curve in the upper diagram along the locus PCC. The Marshallian measurement of the change in consumer's surplus is $P_1 P_2 AB$. This does not normally coincide with any of the four Hicksian measurements. However, if the income elasticity of demand for X is zero, that is if the income effect is zero, then the income consumption curves AC and DB in the upper diagram are vertical. The indifference curves are vertically parallel and have equal slopes for each quantity of X; the income effects, AC and DB in the lower diagram, are zero. The two compensated demand curves coincide with the uncompensated and the triangles AEC and DBF, in the lower diagram, disappear. The assumption of a zero income effect therefore results in the Marshallian measurement representing all four of Hicks' interpretations, and serves in neo-classical analysis the same purpose as the assumption of a constant marginal utility of money in the classical analysis.[1]

The correspondence between the concept of a Paretian optimum and a position from which it is impossible to increase one person's surplus without reducing that of another has already been cited. The Paretian expressions similarly correspond with the definition of a change in surplus as the excess of what an individual is prepared to pay for an additional unit of a good over what he has to pay. MRS measures the former and MRT the latter with respect to any *numéraire*. Equality of MRS and MRT therefore implies that the first order condition for maximizing surplus is satisfied in the case of a pure private good. The aggregate Σ MRS in the case of a public good implies the aggregation of changes in surplus over a number of individuals. The inference that if Σ MRS $>$ MRT the volume of the public good should be increased, if applied to a case where some components of Σ MRS are positive and some negative, suggests that something might be said about a policy change that would leave some persons better off and others worse off. The possibility of extending the analysis to encompass such non-Paretian changes has been the theme of the compensation principle,[2] to which we now turn.

The compensation principle

The concept underlying the compensation principle, generally referred to as the Kaldor–Hicks criterion, is that if a change in policy would result in some persons being better off and some worse off, and the gainers could compensate the losers in such way that on balance everybody was better off, then welfare would be increased by implementing that change. Considerable debate has resulted on the issue of whether it is sufficient that

1. These two assumptions are not quite the same thing, however. A zero income effect only requires that the marginal utility of money be the same for any level of utility no matter what combination of money income and price yields that utility. It is not necessary that the marginal utility of money be the same for different levels of utility.

2. For more detailed accounts of the development of the compensation principle the reader is referred to E. J. Mishan (1964) and I. M. D. Little (1957).

adequate compensation *could* be made or whether it is necessary for the inference that compensation actually be made. Alternative diagrammatic techniques have been developed in the course of the debate, but we shall employ the simplest of these, the utility possibility curves introduced in chapter 3. In a simple two-person model each curve represents the alternate combinations of utility levels that would result from different distributions under one defined set of policies. Two such curves illustrate the possible pairs of utility levels before and after a change in policy. Such diagrams can be interpreted to refer to any change in policy, whether or not its effects are generated through market forces. Where the change consists of a different bundle of goods produced or a different set of prevailing prices, however, it is possible to apply the concept of surplus to assessment of the possibility of compensation.

In Figure 19 point Q_1 represents the existing pair of utility levels and other points along curve Q_1H represent alternate distributions with the existing policies. Point Q_2 represents the position that would be achieved after the policy change in question and other points along Q_2J alternate distributions after the policy change. A change from Q_1 to Q_2 would make person I worse off and person II better off. In Figure 19(a) redistribution from Q_2 to J, after the policy change, would represent compensation of the loser by the gainer. Since at J both persons are better off than at the initial point Q_1, it follows on Paretian grounds that the policy change and compensation would together result in an increase in welfare. In this case the Kaldor–Hicks criterion is satisfied, for there is some point J along the curve through Q_2 that lies north-east of Q_1. In Figure 19(b) the Kaldor–Hicks criterion is not satisfied, but if the policy change were adopted the criterion would be satisfied by a repeal of the policy, for point H, lying on the curve through Q_1, lies north-east of Q_2. Repeal, with compensation for the repeal, would result in a net movement from Q_2 to H, which is a Paretian improvement.

In a case where a policy change affects utility levels through price changes the Kaldor–Hicks criterion can be applied by measurement of consumer's surplus. Figure 19 might represent a case in which the policy change (e.g. membership in a common market) would result in lower prices for some goods and higher prices for others. If person II consumes the former group but not the latter then he would be better off, while if person I consumes only the latter group he would be worse off.

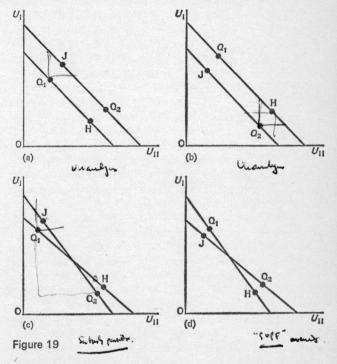

Figure 19

The maximum that person II could pay in compensation while leaving him no worse off would be the compensating variation to him of the price fall, while the minimum amount that person I would have to receive to leave him no worse off would be the compensating variation to him of the price rise. Whether compensation could be paid would then depend on the relative sizes of the compensating variations.

Non-satisfaction of the Kaldor–Hicks criterion does not necessarily mean that the policy change, if adopted, should be repealed. The corresponding criterion then would be whether in the initial position the potential loser could compensate the potential gainer for non-implementation of the policy. Whether such compensation would be possible would depend on the relative magnitudes of the equivalent variations. Scitovsky (1941) demonstrated the possibility that the criterion might be satisfied in both directions, or not satisfied in both directions. These cases are illustrated, respectively, in Figures 19(c) and 19(d) in which the utility possibility curves cross between Q_1 and Q_2. Figure 19(d), for example, would arise if the compensating variation of the price rise for person I exceeded the compensating variation of the price fall for person II, while at the same time the equivalent variation of the price fall for II exceeded the equivalent variation of the price rise for I. Since, as we have seen, in the case of normal goods the equivalent variation of a price fall exceeds the compensating variation, while the compensating variation of a rise exceeds the equivalent variation, this is a definite possibility.

Introduction of the points H and J by the compensation principle in no case enables us to determine the relative welfare levels achieved by points Q_1 and Q_2, for these depend not on whether the constraint (the utility possibility curve) through Q_1 passes north-east or south-west of Q_2, nor on whether the constraint through Q_2 passes north-east or south-west of Q_1, nor any combination of these, but on whether the objective is achieved. This depends on whether the contour of the welfare function through Q_1 passes north-east or south-west of Q_2. If we combine the compensation principle with value judgements on distribution, however, we can derive some meaningful inferences.[1]

If, for example, we assume that perfectly efficient and costless redistribution along either utility possibility curve is feasible, and that the government will always implement the welfare maximizing distribution for any set of policies, then we can

1. For a more exhaustive treatment of the possibilities see Winch (1965).

reason as follows. Since we are initially at Q_1, it follows that this point has been chosen rather than, and is therefore preferred to, H in all four cases. In case (a) the Kaldor–Hicks criterion shows that J is Pareto-preferred to Q_1. If therefore the policy change were implemented together with compensation to achieve J, there would be an increase in welfare. If Q_2 were achieved and no compensation applied, or if redistribution from Q_2 achieved any point on Q_2 other than J, then it would be because such point was distributionally preferred to J and *a fortiori* achieved a higher level of welfare than Q_1. In case (a) we could accordingly conclude that the policy change should be implemented. By similar reasoning we should conclude in case (b) that the change should not be implemented. In case (c) the change should be implemented with compensation, but its implementation without compensation would result in a reduction in welfare, for Q_1 is preferred to H while H is preferred to Q_2. In case (d) we could not tell whether a change without compensation would be an improvement, but could assert that a change with compensation to J would result in a reduction in welfare.

The assumption that redistribution is costless and would always be optimally implemented is an heroic one, but with it we find the Hicksian measurements of the compensating and equivalent variations appropriate criteria to assess policy changes that would affect price levels. If qualities of goods rather than prices would be affected (as for example with rationing schemes), the compensating and equivalent surpluses are similarly relevant. In the real world, however, there are many cases where no attempt would be made to implement compensation. In these cases the Hicksian measurements are inappropriate, for each of them is based on the assumption that the individual is kept on one indifference curve and income effects are completely excluded. If no compensation is made there is an income effect and the magnitude of this affects the value of the change in surplus.

The compensating variation for the price fall was shown in Figure 18 (p. 140) to equal the distance $M_1 M_2$, or the area $P_1 P_2$ AD. This was the amount of money that could be taken from the individual as the price fell so as to leave him neither better nor worse off. If this amount is returned to him, or never taken, and he spends it entirely on other goods, then it is a valid measure of his change in surplus. If the income elasticity of demand for X is positive, however, he will spend part of the compensating variation on X. He then derives additional benefit from the fall in the price of X on those additional units. Only reductions in price below the maximum he would be prepared to pay are relevant, however. That maximum is shown, in the absence of compensation, by the uncompensated demand curve. Thus the additional benefit derived from the price fall on the additional units of X he buys as a result of keeping the compensating variation is shown in the lower part of Figure 18 as the area ADB. When this is added to the compensating variation $P_1 P_2$ AD we have the area $P_1 P_2$ AB as the total measure of the consumer's gain in the absence of compensation.[1] This is, of course, the Marshallian measure of consumer's surplus, but is not dependent on an assumption of either a constant marginal utility of money or a zero income effect. By similar reasoning we see that if we begin with the compensating surplus, the correction is ABF. The triangle DBF that was subtracted from the compensating variation to arrive at the compensating surplus, in recognition of his being required to buy the units $X_4 - X_3$ now has to be added back in, for when he does not lose the compensating variation he chooses to buy these units at OP_1.

The compensating variation for a price rise is equal to the equivalent variation for a price fall and was shown on Figure 18 to equal the area $P_1 P_2$ CB. If the price rose and the consumer received this compensation he would be neither better nor worse off. If this amount were taken back, or never paid, and there was as a result no change in his consumption of X, it would be a valid measure of his loss of surplus from the price rise. A positive income elasticity of demand, however, would result in his purchasing less X if he is not compensated for the price rise. The compensating variation for the price rise

1. For a more detailed development of the concept of consumer's gain see Winch (1965).

included compensation for the increased cost of those units that he would not then buy. It is, of course, appropriate that he should be compensated for the loss of surplus on those sacrificed units, up to the price at which he would refrain from buying them in the absence of compensation. The cut-off price is shown by the uncompensated demand curve AB. But once he has decided not to buy a marginal unit any further increase in its price is irrelevant to him. These further increases are shown by the area ACB. Thus if he does not receive compensation, and accordingly does not buy the last $X_2 - X_1$ units, the compensating variation has over-estimated his loss by ACB. When this is subtracted from $P_1 P_2$ CB we are left with $P_1 P_2$ AB as the measure of his continuing gain from a price fall in the absence of compensation. The compensating surplus for the price rise (the equivalent surplus for the price fall) exceeds the variation by AEC, being the appropriate additional compensation for his not being allowed to purchase $X_2 - X_1$. Since without compensation he would not wish to purchase those units, this item is irrelevant and we are again left with $P_1 P_2$ AB as the measure of an uncompensated loss.

Thus we see that the four Hicksian measurements are completely accurate ways to assess whether the Kaldor–Hicks criterion is satisfied, and that this condition is sufficient for the inference that welfare is increased if full compensation is in fact paid, or is not paid only because some preferred distribution is achieved instead. In such cases there are no problems associated with aggregation, for it is homogeneous dollars of available or necessary compensation that are added and the only question is whether the gainers would in aggregate be prepared to pay sufficient to compensate the losers. Where compensation cannot, or will not, be paid, however, we cannot convert the policy change into a Paretian improvement. Gains and losses will continue to accrue to those experiencing them. These changes in surplus can be measured by the Marshallian measure of consumer's surplus, but such expression in terms of the *numéraire* does not overcome the need for a distributional value judgement.

Simple aggregation of gains and losses will indicate the

direction of a change in welfare if the welfare function registers indifference about the redistribution in utility levels. In many real-world policy issues, where governments attach no significance to the redistributive consequences of a policy change, the Marshallian measure with simple aggregation provides a useful criterion. If the redistributive consequences of the change are judged to be desirable in themselves, then straight aggregation of consumer's surplus will underestimate a net gain or overestimate a net loss. If the aggregate change in surplus is positive we then know that welfare has increased. If, however, the change in surplus is negative we do not know the direction of the change in welfare unless a quantitative judgement is made of how desirable the redistribution is. Similarly if the redistribution is itself considered to be undesirable, then a negative aggregate change in surplus would be sufficient for the inference that adoption of the policy change would reduce welfare, while a positive change would leave us in doubt unless a quantitative judgement concerning the undesirability of redistribution is made. The necessity for a quantitative judgement would itself be evidence that either distribution is currently suboptimal or that compensation should accompany the policy change.

The theory of consumer's surplus and the compensation principle together provide a conceptual framework in which proposed policy changes can be assessed. In practice not all gains and losses will accrue through market changes, and statistical estimation of changes in surplus will not be easy to make. The techniques by which gains and losses, or benefits and costs, can be assessed in practice constitute the technique of cost–benefit analysis, to which we turn in the next chapter.

9 The Practice – Cost–Benefit Analysis

The theory of surplus is concerned with the assessment of the gains and losses, or benefits and costs, that would result from a policy change, and their expression in money. The compensation principle asserts that if the aggregate benefits exceed the aggregate costs, so that it would be possible for the gainers to compensate the losers, then the policy change would yield a net increase in welfare. These are the theoretical foundations of cost–benefit analysis, a technique extensively used in policy analysis, particularly in the appraisal of proposed public works projects. A voluminous literature exists on this subject[1] and we shall be concerned in this chapter only with the basic principles and problems.

The technique is invariably couched in terms of partial equilibrium analysis. It consists of the enumeration and evaluation of a set of consequences of a particular change in the context of a much wider economic environment that remains essentially unaffected. This constant background provides the frame of reference in terms of the value of money that permits benefits and costs to be expressed meaningfully in money. Unless we assume that the marginal utility of money is constant, or that there are zero income effects, even a small change in a single price leads to conceptual imprecision in the use of money as a measuring rod of value. The range of imprecision encompassed within the Hicksian compensating and equivalent variations will be insignificant if the change under analysis is small in relation to the entire economic system. Further problems arise with the use of the Marshallian measure where the prices

1. The interested reader is referred to two excellent surveys, each of which contains extensive further bibliography: Prest and Turvey (1965), and Henderson (1968).

of several things change simultaneously, for the demand curve for each good is prefaced on the assumption that all other prices remain constant. Again the imprecision inherent in simultaneous assessment of several price changes will be insignificant in practice if the entire set of changes is small in relation to the background against which it is assessed. Where the policy under consideration would substantially change the entire economic system it would be necessary to analyse it in a general equilibrium context and no usable body of theory presently exists for such a task. Thus while the basic idea of cost–benefit analysis is as relevant to big changes as to small, the developed techniques of applying the idea are more reliable the smaller the change under consideration. Similarly the basic idea is relevant to any policy change; but its application calls for enumeration and evaluation of effects that can be handled best by available techniques when they manifest themselves in changes in quantities or prices of goods and factors. The techniques, if not the concept, are far more pertinent to an investment in a public utility than to a major social service, the primary effects of which may be intangible. It is for these reasons that cost–benefit analysis has had its widest application in the fields of public works projects and public utilities.

The technique can be applied to a number of questions at different levels, but always involves a comparison of two or more alternatives. The simplest question is whether to undertake a particular project when all the consequences of doing so are known and the only alternative is to remain in the known present position. More common, but less simple, are cases in which a number of alternative projects must be considered simultaneously. It might then be possible to undertake certain combinations of projects but not others. A motorway between two towns could be built to four-lane or six-lane width, but not both, and either could be combined with any one of a number of schemes for urban throughways at each end. The choice of any one project affects the values of benefits and costs on the others. In such a case we are faced not only with the question whether to undertake an improvement, but which set of projects to undertake. Related projects may be implemented sequentially. A four-lane motorway may be built first and the terminal throughways may be worth adding only after traffic volumes have grown. After a further lapse of time the traffic funnelled on to the motorway may make it worth adding additional lanes. In this case we should be concerned not only with which projects to undertake but when to undertake each phase.

The basic criterion of cost—benefit analysis is to maximize benefits in relation to costs. Benefits encompass those consequences of a policy that increase welfare and costs those that reduce it. It follows that the course of action indicated by cost—benefit analysis will be the one from those considered that maximizes welfare. Although simple in concept, application of the criterion gives rise to several problems, both theoretical and statistical. Clearly, there must be some concept of a welfare function so that we can recognize what are benefits and what costs, and what weights attach to each item, yet the function is never explicitly stated by the policy maker. Often the analyst is left to his own devices to state the objective as necessary within the broad confines of the Paretian premises. Where the gains and losses to particular individuals are small in relation to income levels they are normally weighted equally, thereby implicitly assuming that the mild redistribution involved is itself of no consequence. Apart from its simplicity this assumption is of great theoretical and empirical convenience. Where significant gains or losses will accrue to particular individuals or groups the policy maker's attention may be drawn to them, and means suggested whereby they might be offset through pricing or taxation changes.

In some cases the analysis is limited to optimization at a lower level by the specification of the objective in terms of some elements of benefit or cost. Thus the analyst may be asked to recommend the best way to generate a certain amount of electricity, or the best way to create a certain amount of employment in a certain region. In other cases the question of whether to undertake any project is open as well as the question of which project.

Once the objective is at least loosely stated it must be decided what benefits and costs are relevant and how to assess them. It is here that the analyst's command of positive economic theory is crucial. The consequences of each course of action considered must be forecast through time in terms of the effects on quantities and prices of private goods and factors and the volumes of public goods and bads generated. Benefits and costs can be assessed in a number of ways, and great care must be taken to ensure that all significant components are included without double counting. The choice will depend partly on what is considered relevant and partly on what lends itself to ready statistical estimation. A simple example will serve to illustrate the sort of theoretical tangle that must be unravelled and the opportunities for major error that beset the unwary.

Suppose that we are considering the benefits that will accrue from an irrigation project via the growing of corn in a particular area. There is a fixed area of land, agriculture is perfectly competitive, the total product curves of labour before and after irrigation are known, as are the supply curve of labour and demand curve for corn. It is a simple matter to determine the equilibrium levels of labour input, wage level, corn output, corn price and land rent before and after irrigation. Figure 20 illustrates this case, the situation after irrigation being indicated by primes. Rent (R) is shown on the figure in units of corn. Three groups will be affected. Consumers of corn will derive additional consumers' surplus, workers will receive additional factor rents and landowners may receive either higher or lower rents on land. The relevant measurements assuming the supply and demand curves to be linear are;

Rise in consumers' surplus

$$= C(P-P') + \tfrac{1}{2}(P-P')(C'-C) = PABP',$$

Rise in workers' rent

$$= L(W'-W) + \tfrac{1}{2}(W'-W)(L'-L) = WEFW',$$

Rise in land rent

$$= (P'C'-W'L') - (PC-WL)$$
$$= (OP'BC'-OW'FL') - (OPAC-OWEL),$$

Total
$$= (C'-C)\tfrac{1}{2}(P+P') - (L'-L)\tfrac{1}{2}(W+W')$$
$$= CABC' - LEFL'.$$

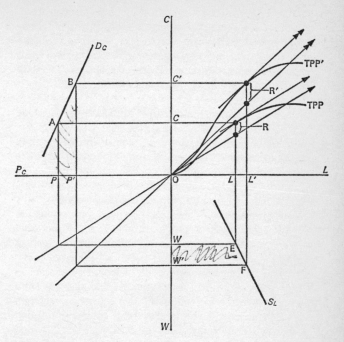

Figure 20

Alternatively we may focus attention not on the changes in surplus but on the changes in output and labour input. Benefit is then the value of the additional corn grown and cost the opportunity cost of the additional labour employed. This approach yields the result

$$\text{Benefit} - \text{cost} = (C'-C)\tfrac{1}{2}(P+P') - (L'-L)\tfrac{1}{2}(W+W')$$
$$= CABC' - LEFL'.$$

It will be seen that both approaches yield the same result. This equality will still hold if other market manifestations are allowed for; the rent on land elsewhere may change, prices of substitute goods may change as may the prices of alternative products of labour. We are faced with the choice between assessing surplus changes generated by price changes and direct valuation of the changes in quantities of outputs and inputs. If the Paretian optimum conditions will be satisfied both before and after the project, as for example if all markets are in perfectly competitive equilibrium, the same aggregate result is achieved either way.

Normally it will be a simpler task empirically to base the calculation on quantity changes. If the distributional effects are likely to be significant, however, then it will be necessary to assess how much each group gains and loses and surpluses must be measured. Measurements based on quantity changes will not indicate, for example, the gains or losses to landowners. Rents could rise or fall. By permitting the aggregate benefits and costs to be assessed by consideration only of the changes in inputs and outputs, the assumption that the redistributional consequences are of no importance is clearly of great practical convenience.

Faulty theory can lead to grossly fallacious, if superficially plausible, assessments. The use of changes in land values as an indicator of benefits is a common case of error. Irrigation increases the productivity of land, but this does not mean that competitive markets will register the benefits as a rise in land values. While the productivity of land rises the effective scarcity of productive land falls. Land values may well fall. Road improvements, by increasing the amount of land of desirable location may well yield great benefits while reducing aggregate land values (see, for example, Winch, 1963). A second plausible error is to add components of surplus to valuation of changes in inputs and outputs. The value of the extra corn less the opportunity cost of the additional labour equals the aggregate change in surplus. We must not then add the surplus caused by the price fall on the previously existing output, nor the wage rise on the previously existing employment. To do so would involve double counting of benefits. Finally, where the product is an intermediate good, we must remember that the demand for it is derived by market forces from the demand for final goods. To add the value of extra bread to the value of extra flour to the value of extra corn would be a clear case of multiple counting.

Real-world cases are, of course, much more complicated than this simple example and great care must be taken in deciding how to approach the measurement of benefits if double counting is to be avoided, nothing is to be missed and the chosen indicators are to be capable of statistical estimation. Any effect generates a stream of market consequences. A benefit that may seem impossible to value at one stage may prove quite tractable at another. Local road improvements, for example, reduce the cost of access to property. These reductions may be difficult to measure directly. If no charge is made for them, however, the benefit will shift to site value where it may readily be assessed. The use of land values as a means for valuing benefits after incidence has shifted, and as a relevant tax base, is quite distinct from the measurement of changes in land value as a separate component of benefit (Winch, 1963). Valuation of time saved and reduced suffering and death caused by road accidents is a difficult problem. Considerable ingenuity has been exercised in devising indirect ways in which values can be placed on such items (Winch, 1963). Where one of the products is a public good, as for example when a dam creates a lake for recreation as well as electric power, irrigation and flood control, the relevant aggregate valuation by users is appropriate but difficult to assess. Again we must use indirect methods to estimate the demand curve (see, for example, Clawson, 1959, and Trice and Wood, 1958).

So far we have assumed that the marginal conditions of Paretian optimality are satisfied both before and after implementation of the project, and that all markets are perfectly competitive. In such a world benefits and costs are in theory clearly defined and projects should be implemented to the stage where a further marginal unit would have a benefit—cost ratio of one. Equality of marginal benefit and marginal cost is simply one of the Paretian conditions of optimality. The real world, however, is far from perfect, and as we saw in the discussion of the theory of second best, if one or more of the marginal conditions is violated it is in general no longer true that the satisfaction of others is desirable. The task of cost–benefit analysis in an imperfect world is to assess a second-best policy, and that is more difficult.

Two alternative corrections to the techniques of cost–benefit analysis are theoretically possible to allow for suboptimality elsewhere in the economy. Following the general theory of second best we could continue to measure benefits and costs in private terms, and assess a cut-off benefit–cost ratio greater or less than one. This would be an approach comparable to the determination of the optimum-price–marginal-cost ratio for a nationalized industry discussed in chapter 6. This technique may be both appropriate and feasible if there is a single constraint of the second-best type. If the aggregate amount of public investment is constrained so that not all worth-while projects can be undertaken simultaneously, for example, variants of this approach may be used to determine which projects should be accorded priority (see, for example, Winch, 1963). We shall return to such cases below. Normally, however, there are numerous constraints of the second-best type throughout the economy and the data requirements for calculation of a single benefit–cost ratio are then so excessive that the technique is not operationally feasible, nor would it be very practical when different projects with different resource requirements and yielding different benefits would have different optimum ratios. The alternative, which is normally adopted, is to retain the cut-off ratio of one, but to allow for suboptimality by assessing social rather than private benefits and costs. In this way the relevant second-best constraints are built into each measurement and it is unnecessary to combine them into a single correction of the ratio. A few examples will illustrate the types of adjustment needed.

Factors employed in the project will normally be diverted from other uses. If all goods were purely private, and price everywhere equal to marginal cost, market prices of the factors diverted would be an accurate indication of opportunity cost. If the factors are diverted from the production of private goods in industries where the price–marginal cost ratio is greater than one, however, factor price will be less than the value of marginal product, and less than opportunity cost. The relevant cost of the project is the value of the alternative product sacrificed and this may necessitate valuing factors above market price in the same ratio as that prevailing between their VMP in alternate uses and market price. Calculation of the appropriate mark-up is essentially the same problem of second-best as that of establishing an appropriate-price—marginal-cost ratio for a nationalized industry. If the alternate use involves public goods or bads, whether as the primary product or through externalities, then assessment of opportunity cost involves assessment of the relevant aggregate marginal valuation. If factor price is used as an indication of cost when the alternative public good is itself underproduced, the result might be the diversion of resources to a worth-while project but from another project that is still more worth-while. Monopsony demand for the output from a project might seriously affect realized benefits. If the crop in the irrigation case previously discussed were sugar beet, we might be tempted to impute a value for the extra crops from the demand for sugar. If the refining industry is a monopoly, however, purchases of beet might be restricted in order to maintain the price of sugar. Irrigation might make it possible to grow additional sugar, but the benefit would not be realized unless the beet is actually grown.

One case where the opportunity cost of a factor might be below market price is one where unemployment presently exists. If the factors that would be used on the project would otherwise be unemployed, opportunity cost would be low. The temptation to assume that if there is any unemployment the real cost of labour is zero must be resisted, however. Projects take time to organize, and short-term unemployment present during the planning phase might have disappeared by the time of implementation. Even if unemployment continues it does not follow that the project will reduce it; factors might in fact be diverted from other uses while the unemployment continues. When there is good reason to expect that a project will absorb factors that would otherwise be unemployed some allowance for that fact is called for. Rather than discount wage costs, however, it might be better to include the alleviation of unemployment among the benefits of the project. This would facilitate direct comparison with alternative employment policies.

Many considerations surround the question of whether inputs and outputs should be valued at market price or price less indirect taxes. Where fuel savings are a significant component of the benefits from a road improvement, the cost of the fuel is clearly relevant, but the fuel tax is a price charged for highway use and should be excluded because it does not represent a saving in real factors. Where an excise tax is imposed on all goods, however, its exclusion from those associated with the project would distort the relevant marginal equivalencies. Clearly the wage cost of labour diverted from other products should not be reckoned net of income tax, for it is gross wage that indicates opportunity cost. A common error in comparisons of road and rail transport costs is failure to correct for the bias caused where railways are liable for property taxes but highways are not. A similar problem arises when land is diverted from taxpaying uses to tax-free highway use. Great care is needed to assess the relevance of taxes in each case, for in a second-best world there are no general rules.

The price or taxation scheme to be used on the project itself might well be critical in cost-benefit analysis. If a swimming pool, for example, were free it might be so congested that little enjoyment would result from its use (see chapter 7). It might then not be worth building. If an appropriate admission charge were made, however, to allow for the externalities generated by marginal users, benefits might well exceed costs. Conversely if existing pools are already overcongested because free, the relief of congestion by building another pool might result in benefits exceeding costs. If present congestion were relieved by appropriate admission charges, however, the additional pool might not be worth building. Though more complicated, similar considerations clearly apply to highway construction.

161 - + # NPV JIRR

The problem of time

Most projects assessed by cost–benefit analysis have long anticipated lives. Characteristically, initial construction costs are high and subsequent operating costs low, while benefits may continue evenly or grow through time. Costs and benefits can be dated and costs will typically exceed benefits at first while benefits exceed costs later. These are the normal features of any investment. An overall assessment of the relationship between benefits and costs necessitates an appropriate discounting procedure. Two methods are in common use and considerable controversy surrounds their relative merits. The present-value method involves use of an explicit rate of discount. The excess of benefits over costs is first assessed for each period in the future. At first when costs exceed benefits this will be negative. The net benefit for each period is then discounted at the explicit interest rate to yield a present value, and the sum of these present values is the present value (PV) of the project. If PV is positive the present value of the anticipated future stream of benefits exceeds that of the anticipated stream of costs. The internal rate of return (RR) avoids use of an explicit interest rate by calculating that rate at which the stream of net benefits will discount to a present value of zero. If we lived in a first-best world and knew the appropriate rate of interest, and all decisions were of the simple type whether or not to undertake a particular project, there would be no problem. A project would be worth undertaking if either $PV > 0$ or $RR > i$. Both methods would always give the same result. When we relax these idealistic assumptions and consider the real world, however, they are not equivalent and each gives rise to difficulties.

The major difficulty with the present-value technique is that calculation cannot be undertaken until the appropriate interest rate is decided. In an imperfect world a number of different interest rates may exist simultaneously and the choice among them will depend upon both the anticipated opportunity cost of the capital invested in the project, and upon value judgements. If resources for the project will be diverted from other forms of government expenditure, and the interest rate on government bonds is considered to represent the rate of return on marginal government expenditure, then use of that rate will result in optimum resource allocation within the government investment sector. Resource allocation may be suboptimal between that sector and others, however. If the project would be financed by a bond issue by a public corporation and it is assumed that resources for it would be diverted from investment in the private sector, then the relevant rate of interest is the marginal rate of return in private investment, for this represents the opportunity cost of the project. Similar reasoning holds if the project is tax-financed to the extent that increased taxation results in lower investment in the private sector. Where the effect would be reduced consumption, however, the matter is more difficult, for the relevant rate then is not an alternative rate of return but a rate of time preference. There is no single rate of interest in the real world that reflects the time preference of the public. Small savers may lend at much lower rates than debtors pay on consumer credit. To assess the appropriate rate statistically we should need to know whose consumption is reduced. A much deeper problem is raised by the argument that existing market interest rates reflect only private time preference while the relevant rate would be a rate of social time preference. We shall return to that argument below, for it raises the question not merely of whether the proposed project would optimize the allocation of a given level of investment, but of whether that level is itself optimal and, if not, whether it should be changed by implementation of the proposed project. So difficult are the problems associated with selection of an appropriate interest rate that cost–benefit analysts often avoid them, either by repeating the calculations for a number of sample rates or by calculating the internal rate of return, thereby leaving it to the policy maker to select the appropriate rate.

The internal rate of return technique has the great practical advantage that it postpones decision on the appropriate interest rate until after the calculations are made. Some decision must, of course, be made eventually, for decision to implement the project implies that the relevant rate is below the internal rate of return. How much below need never be decided, however, so that if the rate of return is high the contentious issue of just how high the relevant interest rate is need never be faced. Similarly if the rate of return is low and the project rejected, all that is implied is that whatever the relevant rate is, it is above that figure. If the rate of return is within the contentious range, however, the issue must be faced. Thus for simple cases where the only question is whether or not to proceed with a particular project, use of the internal rate of return might avoid much irrelevant debate concerning the relevant rate of interest.

Where the project is of such nature that it may be undertaken on alternative scales the problem is less simple. It is not then sufficient to calculate a rate of return for each scale. The smallest scale would probably show the highest rate of return and larger scales may descend in sequence. These, however, would be average rates of return, while the relevant criterion is the marginal rate of return on each incremental step. Because the smallest scale has the highest rate does not mean that it is the best choice. Subsequent increments may yield high enough rates of return to be worth undertaking. Where the scale of the project is finely divisible and the marginal rate of return falls steadily, choice of the best scale requires definition of the relevant rate of interest within narrow bounds, for the decision on scale implies that the relevant interest rate is below the marginal rate of return on the last increment built, but above that on the next. If the present-value technique is used it is, of course, again necessary to calculate the present values of successive marginal increments.

While sufficient for the choice of whether to undertake a project, and if so on what scale, the internal rate of return is less satisfactory where a choice must be made among mutually exclusive alternatives. Two alternative plans may have equal capital outlays initially. One may yield high benefits at first and low benefits later, while the other may yield higher benefits later. Both might have the same internal rate of return, but that does not mean that we should be indifferent between them.

The relative valuation of future benefits will depend on the rate of discount, not the rate of return. It is therefore quite possible that a project yielding earlier benefits will show the higher rate of return, while if discounted at an interest rate significantly below the rate of return on either project, the one with later returns would have the greater present value. In such a case it will also be relevant to know whether the earlier benefits will be reinvested and if so at what rate of return. One particular form of choice among mutually exclusive alternatives concerns the best time to implement a project. With traffic volumes growing through time, a road improvement becomes worth-while at some stage. Cost–benefit analysis may be used to indicate whether it is worth undertaking now, next year or some year thereafter. With an appropriate discount rate the present-value technique accurately reflects the lower present value of postponed capital expenditure. This the internal rate of return does not show, for it avoids decision on the crucial issue of the rate of discount that determines the significance attaching to postponement. With the internal rate of return technique we should have to calculate first the rate of return on immediate implementation and then the internal marginal rate of return on each possible period of postponement. Since time is divisible this would involve a great deal of calculation that would be avoided by use of the present value, and in such a case it would in any case be necessary to specify the relevant rate of discount, eventually, when deciding on the best time for implementation.

Thus, while the internal rate of return may obviate the need for precise definition of the relevant interest rate in questions concerning whether to undertake an investment, it has severe shortcomings when the issue is which project to undertake or when to implement it. The present-value technique overcomes these problems, but only if the appropriate interest rate is precisely specified.

We have so far discussed choice of an appropriate interest rate in a second-best context where the objective is to achieve a second-best optimum allocation of a given amount of investment within the public and private sectors. The optimum aggregate level of investment is a different problem. It has been argued that if market interest rates reflect anything it is a private expression of time preference. Individuals, it is argued, discount the future too much, partly because their life expectancy is short and uncertain and they might not live to enjoy a postponed benefit, and partly because if they do live long enough they expect to be too old to enjoy it. Neither of these considerations applies to society as a whole. Growth in the standard of living, combined with the classical assumption of diminishing marginal utility, would justify a positive rate of time preference for both the individual and society, however. On balance it is contended the social rate of time preference should be lower than the private rate.

A quite different argument for a lower social rate of time preference has been advanced by Marglin (1963). Each member of society might be asked to weight the significance he attaches to a marginal unit of real income for other members of his own generation and for members of future generations. If he discounts for futurity at a rate lower than the marginal productivity of investment, then he would advocate that others invest more. He might, however, attach a much higher weight to his own real income than to other members of his own generation and accordingly be unwilling to invest more himself. Each person may be in this position, so that if the decision to save and invest is a purely private one no more will be saved. If, however, all were forced to save and invest more, all would agree that it was a good thing if the benefit derived from seeing real income transferred from the many other members of one's own generation to future generations aggregated to more than the loss incurred by having some of one's own real income transferred. With assumed weights the optimal rate of time preference is readily calculated. Thus, while additional saving would not be considered worth while by each person acting alone, it might be considered worth while by all, acting together. In such a case the social rate of discount would be below any private rate.

While it is difficult to fault the logic of this argument it is necessarily based on theoretical premises that give rise to considerable problems. If a reduction in the real income of one person is to be offset in its impact on his utility by a transfer of real income from other members of his own generation to members of future generations, then it is necessary that all individuals' real income levels enter the utility function of each. This requires that utility functions be interdependent in the sense that a change in the quantities of goods and services available to one person will make others feel better- or worse-off by reason of their feelings of altruism or envy. This is an inter-relationship among utility functions quite different from the generation by one person's consumption of externalities in commodity space in the form of local public goods and bads. To enjoy the beauty of the flowers in my neighbour's garden is a purely selfish matter quite compatible with independent utility functions. For me to feel better off because my neighbour is enjoying a good dinner is another matter. Traditionally welfare economics is based on the assumption that utility functions are independent, and considerable analytical complexity is avoided by this assumption. From the assumption of independence, however, it follows that each person attaches zero importance to the real incomes of others of all generations so that the Marglin effect cannot arise. To consider his argument as a possibly valid reason for adopting a low rate of social time preference in cost–benefit analysis forces us to reconsider the very foundations on which Paretian welfare economics is built.

There are strong grounds for arguing that to be either realistic or consistent welfare economics should be based on the assumption that utility functions are interdependent. To assume that a society adopts the Paretian value judgement, that if one person is better off and others no worse off there is an increase in welfare, while at the same time assuming that each member of the society is totally indifferent to the well-being of others is hardly consistent. To require the welfare function of a society to encompass distributional value judgements while each member is totally indifferent to the pattern of distribution among others is equally unsatisfactory. These assumptions force us to postulate a welfare function that is defined for the society by some government, without being derived from the feelings of equity prevalent among the members of that society, for by the assumption of independent utility functions the members have no such feelings. Quite apart from its logical inconsistency the assumption of independence lacks credibility as a realistic description of the society in which we live. Individuals are prepared to support schemes of income redistribution, tax-financed education, etc., that impose upon them sacrifices that they would not voluntarily make from motives of charity.[1] Such behaviour is quite consistent with the interdependent utility functions implicit in the Marglin argument, but can hardly be reconciled with the conventional premises.

Quite apart from the added complexity, the assumption of interdependence of utility functions has been avoided by welfare economists largely because of the difficulties to which it gives rise. If we accept that the real incomes of others may be weighted positively in the utility function, there is no reason why they should not be weighted negatively. Envy is as strong an emotion as altruism. But if sufficiently strong negative weights are allowed, then all may be better off if the real income of each is reduced. One's gloating over the deprivation of others may offset the hardships of one's own poverty. If utility is dependent not so much on one's own real income, as on the relative level of one's own income to others, then growth may be self-defeating as a route to increased happiness. With appropriate weights interdependent utility functions may make possible cases in which a redistribution of real income would make all better off. A low social rate of time preference and schemes to reduce the inequality of incomes may then constitute Paretian improvements, but, as we shall see in the next

1. An interesting case of 'collective charity' arises in the North American institution of the United Appeal. While donations are voluntary, individuals are subjected to considerable social pressure to give a 'fair' share. Individuals may then be willing to give because, and only because, they believe all will be coerced into giving. Where charity is an individual matter a person may give more the less others give, because his donation is then more important. With the Marglin effect inherent in collective charity he may give more the more others give, because his own sacrifice is then more acceptable.

chapter, there is in general no unique corresponding concept of an optimum distribution. Even with interdependent utility functions it is still necessary to impose some concept of equity by a welfare function encompassing distributional value judgements that are not derived from the utility functions themselves. Since interdependence does not obviate the need for this exogenously postulated objective, its additional complexity has traditionally been rejected in favour of the simpler assumption of independence.

Thus we see that the case for a low social rate of time preference in cost–benefit analysis goes to the very root of the value premises on which welfare economics is based. It is not surprising that it has proved to be a controversial issue. The appropriate rate of interest and the optimum rate of growth are interdependent for any marginal productivity of investment. If a government is prepared to select either by value judgement, the other can be deduced from it. Both depend on the distributional value judgements inherent in the welfare function as these relate the utility levels of present and future generations. To what extent a government is responsible for the welfare of future generations is a deep philosophical issue. It cannot be resolved democratically, for the votes of the unborn cannot be recorded. Even if they could we would not know what weight to attach to them, and if that question were answered we should still be faced with the logical problem of deriving social choice from individual values that is the subject of the next chapter.

The escape from this impasse, as far as the applied world of cost–benefit analysis is concerned, is simple. Even if the case for a social rate of time preference below market interest rates were sound, its use is a criterion for public investment, while private time preference governs private investment, would distort the allocation of capital. If a higher level of investment and faster rate of growth is warranted, it could be achieved with optimal allocation only by the use of monetary and fiscal policy to reduce market interest rates for all investment purposes. Cost–benefit analysis can only assess a particular project in the context of such parametric constraints of the entire economy.

Some final problems

In a first-best Paretian world, optimality is determined by the welfare function, utility functions and the transformation function. In the real world, however, the cost–benefit analyst may be faced with a number of constraints of the second-best type as well as the real economic constraint inherent in the transformation function. One cannot use cost–benefit analysis to achieve a perfect world, but only to improve the fit of one piece of an imperfect jigsaw puzzle. There may be constraints imposed by law. The procedures laid down for compulsory purchase of land, for example, may preclude the ready achievement of optimum land use patterns. The administrative machinery within which decisions are made and implemented may be far from perfect, and statistical analysis is not a free good. The analyst may have to make do with poor data and inadequate resources for analysis. Greater precision in the analysis of one project may then make it impossible to consider another project at all. The best quality of analysis must be determined in the light of such constraints and may well fall short of the precision that is theoretically possible. Sensitivity tests are a useful way to focus resources on the most important items for more detailed study. Budgetary constraints may limit the range of possible alternatives. The aggregate amount that a government is willing to invest may fall short of the optimum amount, and in some jurisdictions there may be constitutional limitations on levels of government indebtedness that make it impossible to implement all worth-while projects. Time lags in adjustment of the private sector may make it necessary to postpone certain projects that are apparently worth undertaking immediately. Simultaneous implementation of a number of construction projects designed to catch up on accumulated backlog may severely overtax the existing capacity of the construction industry. Delays and higher costs would result while the industry expands to a size that may result in unemployment once the crash programme is terminated. In such cases projects must be phased through time by judicious apportioning of priorities.

Various other objectives of policy may be imposed on the cost–benefit analyst in the form of constraints. He may be required to assess benefits on the assumption that a break-even pricing system will be used, even though it is suboptimal. In principle he can be limited to those solutions that are compatible with a target level for the achievement of almost any apparently irrelevant dimension of overall government policy.

Finally we must remember that the analyst works in a world that is beset not only by imperfections but by uncertainties. Forecasts are notoriously unreliable, and the longer the life of the project the further into the future must forecasts be made and the greater will be the uncertainties attaching to them. How to allow for uncertainty will depend on value judgements concerning risk aversion. Calculations may be based on the most likely single outcome, which maximizes the proportion of cases in which the forecast is correct, or they may be based on mean probabilities, which balances overestimates and underestimates. Where inaccuracy of the forecast or the emergence of an outcome to which only a low probability attaches would have disastrous consequences, a minimum regret constraint may be imposed. In water resource projects, for example, divergencies from expectations are not self-balancing. Too little water is a drought and too much a flood, and equal probabilities of drought and flood do not constitute a mean expectation of ideal water levels. The best project may then be not the one that on average yields the best water level but the one that minimizes the variations in water level.

Any project is assessed against the background of a given economic environment, but that environment changes exogenously through time. The projected life of a project is not its anticipated physical life but its predictable useful life, as many quite serviceable but abandoned railway tunnels bear witness. How conditions will change in the future is never accurately known. Technology changes, tastes change and the welfare function changes. In some cases future benefits may be subjected to a higher discount rate as a risk premium to allow for uncertainty, but this simple expedient falls far short of adequately allowing for all the ramifications of uncertainty. When the future is uncertain, a project that will be flexible and adaptable to a wide range of conditions may be a wiser choice even though it will not be the optimum project for any particular set of conditions. It may be better to be sure that the chosen project will be slightly suboptimal than run the risk of its proving to be grossly inappropriate.

The alternative techniques of allowing for uncertainty are many and cannot be fully considered here. Where there is uncertainty a second-best outcome is not calculable. Where the future is unknown we are reduced to a third-best world of deriving what guidance we can from such information as we have about the best way to use the power at our disposal. This is an imprecise business, but the real world does not conform to the niceties of a simplified analytical model. For all its imperfections, imprecision and scope for controversy, cost–benefit analysis remains the most useful technique we have for focusing attention on the crucial issues involved in making decisions that must be made somehow. As Prest and Turvey (1965, p. 700) so aptly remarked, 'The truth of the matter is that, whatever one does, one is trying to unscramble an omelette, and no one has yet invented a uniquely superior way of doing this.'

Part Four The Politics of Social Choice

10 The Politics of Social Choice

Throughout the discussion of welfare economics in previous chapters, we have assumed that there exists a social welfare function. The focus of attention has been the process of maximizing that objective in the presence of various constraints, and the properties and corollaries of the optimum solution. The subject has been built on the foundation of maximization theory, employing the techniques of marginal geometry and differential calculus. This whole edifice has relevance only if there is meaning to the concept of collective rationality, for unless there is some definable objective that a society seeks to achieve it is meaningless to inquire into the method of pursuing it.

That individuals have goals is intuitively self-evident, for without goals there can be no concept of motivation, still less of rational behaviour. The concept of a common objective for a society as a group is more contentious, however. It is not our task in this book to examine in depth the philosophical issues raised by the concept of social purpose; but it is incumbent upon us, if welfare economics is to have any usefulness, to enquire into the possible, and impossible, ways in which a welfare function may be formulated, and the logical consistency of Paretian welfare economics with the alternate forms that such a function might have.

The welfare function may in principle originate in any of three sources. It may be determined from outside the society itself and be imposed upon it. Whether such a function represents the will of God, Superman or a dictator, the formal analytics of maximizing it are straightforward once it is known, for the process is simply that of maximizing the objective of the single source, whatever it may be. Alternatively the objective may derive from the common instinct of the members of the society itself. In both of these cases there is absence of conflict, the common purpose is either imposed upon the society or recognized by all without dispute. The third case is that in which the purpose of the group is in some way distilled from their divergent private objectives. This is the model of the democratic society in which consensus somehow emerges from conflict.

If we assume that the relevant source of the welfare function for our purposes is the conflicting goals of the members of the society themselves, then it is necessary that there be some mechanism by which differences can be resolved and a single set of goals be determined that it is the aim of the society as a whole to achieve. Conflict will always result in an outcome, but this alone does not constitute a goal. The present state of the society in which we live is the outcome of millenia of human conflict, but that does not mean that it is optimal. Welfare economics is meaningful only if there is an objective that might or might not be achieved, or might be capable of different degrees of achievement. In a democratic society that objective, the welfare function, must be distilled from the divergent opinions of its members through a political process.

The mechanism by which conflict is resolved into consensus is a constitution. The constitution is a set of rules by which the conflicting opinions of many are resolved into a social choice. To be viable the constitution must be accepted by all members as a fair set of rules of the game, so that all will accept the outcome even though it may not accord with the private preferences of some. Such a concept is inherent in the rule of law and the social contract. Many forms of constitution have been conceived, and a diversity exists in the world today. Debate on their relative merits is endless. One recent contribution to this debate of fundamental importance is Arrow's (1963) 'General Possibility Theorem', a rigorous demonstration of the impossibility of devising a constitution that will have certain apparently desirable attributes.

The impossibility of a 'perfect' constitution

That simple-majority rule has limitations of a theoretical as well as a practical kind has long been recognized. The simplest case in which it breaks down is the well-known paradox of voting. Let three persons rank three alternatives in order of preference. Their ballots might show

	Mr A	Mr B	Mr C
1st choice	X	Y	Z
2nd choice	Y	Z	X
3rd choice	Z	X	Y

There is now a two-to-one majority in favour of X over Y, Y over Z and Z over X. The outcome is intransitive. If a single vote is first taken to choose between two alternatives, and a second vote then taken between the outcome so selected and the third possibility, we find that whichever outcome is omitted from the first vote emerges as the one selected.

Various more complex schemes of voting have been devised in an attempt to overcome the breakdown of simple-majority rule when a choice must be made from among more than two alternatives. In his general possibility theorem, Arrow shows that no such scheme could possibly be devised that would satisfy two axioms and five conditions. The two axioms simply require connectivity and transitivity. Connectivity means that the scheme will yield a relation of either social preference or indifference between every possible pair of alternatives; it will never fail to yield a result. Transitivity means that if X is preferred to Y and Y to Z, then X is preferred to Z. The preference for X over Z also holds if either prior relation is one of indifference, while if there is indifference both between X and Y and between Y and Z then there must be indifference between X and Z. The axioms together require that the system of social decision making yields complete and consistent results. The five conditions on those results imposed by Arrow are more restrictive although still such as to meet with widespread acceptance.

The first condition requires that there be a set of three alternatives which individuals are free to order in any way. The proof that no scheme exists that will result in a true social ordering for three alternatives implies that no scheme could order three of many alternatives, and could not therefore completely order a set of more than three alternatives. The second condition of positive association between social and individual values is similar to the Paretian value judgement. It requires that 'if one alternative social state rises or remains still in the ordering of every individual without any other change in those orderings, . . . then it rises, or at least does not fall, in the social ordering.' (Arrow, 1963). The third condition, independence of irrelevant alternatives, requires that the social ordering of any two outcomes shall not be influenced by the presence of any other alternatives in the set to be ordered. If three possibilities are considered, X, Y and Z, and individuals rank these in order of preference, then each individual's ordering of X and Y would be the same as if he had been asked to order a set containing only X and Y or containing X, Y, Z and W. Wherever he places Z and W in his order of preference will not affect the relative positions of X and Y. Condition three requires that the social ordering of X and Y depend solely on the individual orderings of X and Y regardless of whether Z or W, or neither or both, are included in the set being ordered. The fourth condition, citizens' sovereignty, requires that the social ordering shall not be imposed upon the society. The social ordering of any pair of alternatives shall not be the same regardless of individual orderings. This condition simply requires that the social ordering shall be dependent on, and in some way be derived from, individual orderings. The final condition is that of non-dictatorship, which requires that the social ordering shall not coincide with the ordering of any particular individual regardless of the ordering of others. Thus condition four requires that the social choice shall not be imposed from outside the society, while five requires that it shall not be imposed by one person inside the society. Together they require that the social ordering must in some way be derived from the possibly conflicting orderings of different individuals.

The proof[1] of the theorem rests on the concept of a decisive set. A set of voters is decisive in establishing a social preference for X over Y if their ranking of X as preferred to Y is sufficient

1. The outline of the proof given here includes only the salient features. For a complete and rigorous proof of the theorem the reader is referred to Arrow (1963).

to establish a corresponding social ordering, regardless of the ordering of those outcomes by other individuals. Let V be the smallest of all the decisive sets,[1] and let it be decisive for X against Y. V is subdivided into V_1, a single individual in V, and V_2 all other members of V; while V_3 represents all persons not in V.[2] Suppose the individual orderings are as follows:

V_1 ranks X preferred to Y preferred to Z,
V_2 all rank Z preferred to X preferred to Y,
V_3 all rank Y preferred to Z preferred to X.

Now V_1 and V_2 (that is all members of V) rank X preferred to Y and, since V is defined as decisive for X against Y, this is sufficient to establish the social ordering X preferred to Y. Persons in V_2 rank Z preferred to Y while all others prefer Y to Z. If the social ordering were Z preferred to Y, V_2 would be decisive for that choice. But V_2 is one member smaller than the smallest decisive set and cannot therefore be decisive for anything. It follows that Z is not socially preferred to Y and therefore that Y is either preferred to or indifferent to Z. By the axiom of transitivity it follows that X is socially preferred to Z. Since all persons other than V_1 prefer Z to X, however, this implies that V_1 is a dictator. This proves that it is impossible for any system of social decision making to satisfy both axioms and all five conditions.

Examination of the axioms and conditions of Arrow's theorem shows various ways in which a system of social decision making might be devised that will satisfy all but one of them. The choice of which to relax is not as arbitrary as might at

1. The decisive set for X against Y might not be the same as for Y against X. If X is the status quo, Y some proposed change, and a two-thirds majority is required to implement a change, then the decisive set for Y against X is twice as large as that for X against Y.

2. V_1 cannot be an empty set for that would imply that V is empty, which would violate condition four. V_2 cannot be empty for that would imply that V_1 is a dictator for X over Y and it can be shown that this implies that V_1 is a dictator for all choices, which violates condition five. V_3 cannot be empty for V would then require unanimity for X against Y, in which case one person is decisive for Y against X, which violates condition five.

first sight appear, however. If the axiom of connectivity is relaxed we cannot have a complete system, for it would be incapable of making choices between some outcomes in some circumstances. Relaxation of the axiom of transitivity permits social choice to run around in circles, for whatever policy was adopted there would be some preferred policy to adopt instead. Relaxation of the first condition would limit the scope of the system to cases in which there was a certain measure of consensus among the citizenry, leaving unresolved the most difficult cases where opinions conflict. To relax either condition four or five would be incompatible with the commonly held concept of democracy, and would still leave unanswered the basic problems of choosing the outside authority or inside dictator in whom authority for social decision making would rest. Attention has accordingly been focused on conditions two and three as those offering the most promising prospect of an escape from the impasse.

Conditions two and three together require that social preferences be derived entirely from the ordinal preferences of individuals. No account is taken either of the strength of preferences held by a single individual for some alternatives over others or of the relative strengths of preference that hold among individuals. This is in strict accordance with the neo-classical concept that utility is purely ordinal. Arrow's theorem, however, shows that strictly ordinal private preferences are not sufficient for the determination of social choice in the context of the axioms and other conditions. If utility were an objectively measurable, inter-personally comparable, cardinal magnitude then the maximization of aggregate utility would constitute the basis for a complete social ordering of social states. Such a concept of utility would overcome the two basic shortcomings of any system based on purely ordinal preferences. Individuals would have some way of indicating, or having assessed, their strengths of preference, and a weighting system would exist whereby the preferences of different individuals could be combined with appropriate weight. Any system of social decision making must somehow come to grips with these two problems, and we shall consider them in turn.

Individual strength of preference

That the political problem of social choice should be insoluble without some means whereby individuals can indicate strength of preference should come as no surprise to economists, for no system of resource allocation, through the market or otherwise, could function efficiently without such a mechanism. Consider, for example, the simple case of an agricultural community faced with the problem of how to allocate orchard land among the growing of apples, plums and pears. If we

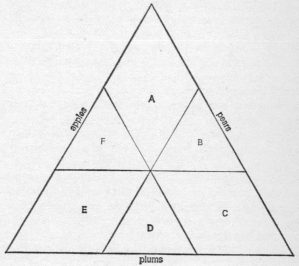

Figure 21

assume that the total area of land is fixed, the problem is to determine how many acres should be devoted to each type of fruit. This case is illustrated in Figure 21, which consists of an equilateral triangle the height of which represents the fixed area of land on a linear scale. Any point within the triangle represents the allocation of land to the three crops, the amount going to each being indicated by the length of the perpendicular from that point to the relevant side. The sum of the three perpendiculars must always equal the height of the triangle. If each of three voters has a different favourite fruit, and does not like the other two, each will vote for any reallocation of land that lengthens the perpendicular to the side representing his own favourite fruit and against any that shortens it. In Figure 21 lines through the present allocation parallel to the sides divide all possible reallocations into six zones. There will be a two-to-one majority for reallocations into zones B, D and F (i.e. those bounded by one side) and against reallocations into zones A, C and E (i.e. those bounded by two sides). Clearly there can be no equilibrium. If all voters like all types of fruit we could replace the straight lines through the existing allocation by indifference curves for the three persons. There would now be an equilibrium if the bliss points of any two or all three indifference maps coincided, or if the bliss point of one coincided with tangency between indifference curves of the other two. In general the probability of there being a determinate outcome is remote.

While apparently irresolvable politically, this allocation problem is readily solved by free competitive markets. Each person expresses his preferences through his demand prices for the various forms of fruit. The cardinal properties of money can stand as proxy for a cardinal measure of utility, and even money can be dispensed with in theory by use of the cardinal properties of fruit expressed in common marginal rates of substitution between any pair. The weighting of each person's preferences is determined partly by his taste for fruit relative to other goods and partly by his income. Such a system has been referred to as dollar votes in the market. It relies on some exogenously determined distribution of voting strength (income) and a mechanism (exchange) whereby 'votes' can be used to indicate strength of preference.

Some interesting analogues of the exchange process have been developed in theories of political decision making (see, for example, Coleman, 1966, Winch, 1969). The most direct analogue is the practice of vote trading or 'log rolling', which is alleged to be a common practice in some legislative bodies. The initial distribution of power is laid down by the constitution and normally each legislator has one vote on each issue. Each legislator will feel more strongly about some issues than others, however, and their relative strengths of preferences might be different. If legislator A feels more strongly about issue X than issue Y, while B is more concerned about Y than X, they may trade votes. This is normally accomplished by an informal agreement by which A agrees to vote B's way on issue Y and B to vote A's way on X. The development of a perfect market in vote trading is often hampered by the common feeling that such practices are underhanded and contrary to the spirit of the constitution. If free exchange were openly and efficiently organized, however, there could exist a market equilibrium set of exchange ratios for votes on different issues. From the barter equilibrium it would be a small step to develop a *numéraire*. Each legislator could be issued with coupons with which he could buy votes on different issues, the coupon allowance being just sufficient to purchase one vote on each issue if he so chose. Instead he could purchase more votes on issues about which he was most concerned and none on others. A free market would readily establish the highest coupon prices for votes on the most contentious issues. While in the real world such practices are normally limited to a primitive form of barter it can be shown that in theory they lead to outcomes that are Pareto superior to the outcome if each legislator acts independently (Coleman, 1966).

Another common way in which strengths of preference are brought to bear in the political process is through the use of pressure and propaganda (see Breton, 1966). A government can be subjected to considerable influence by pressure groups. The assumption that the effectiveness of political pressure will be directly related to the efforts devoted to it, which in turn are directly related to the strength of motivation, leads to the conclusion that where social choices are influenced by pressure the outcome will be Pareto superior to that if no such practice prevails (Winch, 1969). Similar arguments hold with respect to propaganda. The common feature of all such systems is that some mechanism exists whereby individuals can express not merely the direction of their preference but the strength of that preference. They vary considerably in efficiency, however, for in some the expression is virtually costless in resource terms while in others the very medium of expression is a willingness to spend resources thereon. Devices of similarly different efficiency are in use in markets for private goods, where the problem is comparable. At times it is virtually impossible to rationalize the mix of techniques adopted by a society.

Economic theory has demonstrated that if the distribution of income is equitable, free exchange on competitive markets is a very efficient way to distribute scarce private goods among individuals. What might normally be considered a satisfactory basis for the equitable distribution of income might be unacceptable in abnormal times, however. Thus, during the second world war when food was in abnormally short supply, free markets would have resulted in such high food prices that the poor would have been in danger of starvation. The system of distribution was temporarily modified by redefining the distribution of income in terms of scarce commodities by the issue of ration coupons. Each person was entitled to, and restricted to, the purchase of so much meat, so much butter, etc. at controlled low prices. Having overcome the temporary unacceptability of the pattern of income distribution in this way, however, the system went further and prohibited individuals from benefiting by free exchange. It was illegal to exchange meat coupons or butter coupons for non-rationed goods by a simple sale of coupons for money. At the same time that free exchange was prohibited for some goods, advantage of it was taken for others. The 'points' rationing scheme for a wide range of goods involved the issue of a second currency, 'points', and points prices as well as money prices were controlled for the goods covered by the scheme. Points prices were frequently adjusted to raise the price of popular goods and reduce that of less popular goods so as to equate demand to available supplies. The rational use of the exchange mechanism to approximate Pareto optimality over one range of goods coexisted with its prohibition for another range of goods, coupled with severe penalties for 'black market' activities.

In this inconsistency there is a close parallel with the attitude that vote trading is immoral in a society that normally practises free exchange.

Another common practice where the pattern of income distribution is considered inequitable for certain scarce goods is trial by queueing. The cheapest seats at the Royal Opera House in London are priced below market levels, so that the poor may have the opportunity to attend. The seats are allocated to those with the strongest preferences, strength of preference being indicated by the number of hours or nights one is prepared to sit on the pavement in a queue before the box office opens. Such practices have a long history in primitive societies, other examples being the allocation of scarce princesses to the knights who slay most dragons and the allocation of high political office to the candidate most willing to exhaust himself on campaign tours before assuming the burdens of office. The pressure group system in politics works the same way, the greatest weight being attached to the preferences of those prepared to expend most effort and resources in demonstrating their concern. However romantic the stories of the labours of Hercules, the economist will recognize that different forms of expression of strength of preference vary considerably in their efficiency. Free exchange is relatively costless, but some methods actually measure strength of preference by the volumes of resources expended in expressing them. Student demonstrators occasionally express strength of feeling by the volume of other people's property they are prepared to expend to attract attention.

Thus we find that while Arrow's model demonstrates the impossibility of making social choices on the basis of individuals' orders of preference alone, and therefore indicates the need for some means by which individuals can express relative strengths of preference; in the real world a host of such means has been developed. Their crucial role in the political process is hampered, however, by traditional attitudes of political morality; just as the role of interest rates in establishing an optimum pattern of investment was once hampered by the belief that usury was a sin. There remains the problem of weighting the preferences expressed, and this is essentially the problem of distribution to which we now turn.

Weighting of individual preferences

Whatever the medium through which an individual expresses the relative intensities of his various desires, any comparison among individuals will depend upon their initial endowment of the relevant medium. In a state of anarchy, where the law of the jungle prevails, each individual is free to fight hardest for those things that concern him most, and the natural weighting of different individuals' preferences rests on their initial endowments of brute strength and native cunning. The development of orderly human society is the story of the replacement of brute strength by other media for the expression of preferences. Supremacy won in combat became the divine right of kings, the rule of force became the rule of law and the spoils of past conflict became the institution of private property. The right of an individual to whatever his native talents could wrest from a hostile natural environment became the labour theory of value, and is in turn the basis in natural law for the alleged equity of that pattern of distribution resulting from the pricing of factors according to their marginal productivities that is inherent in the perfectly competitive general equilibrium.

Groups are more powerful than individuals. Cohesive societies arise where all members of a group are prepared to exchange recognition of the rights of others within the group to some pattern of distribution for protection by the group from persons outside it. So great are the advantages of membership in such a society that internal cohesion may be possible for a wide range of distributions. Once established, the existing distribution of rights may change only in deference to a threat of internal revolution or as a result of internal disorder or war between societies. Voluntary membership of such a society is the basis of the concept of the social contract. The stability of a society, system of government, or pattern of distribution, does not rest on its being in any sense based on an optimal set of value judgements, but rather on its being not sufficiently unacceptable to a sufficient number of persons for them to be willing to undertake the considerable efforts necessary to effect a change. The essence of stability is not perfection but friction. A government in power may be able to pursue a wide range of alternate policies and still win the next election. The leader of such a party could enforce his own preferences within wide limits before others are prepared to make the effort necessary to depose him. The range of possibilities open to a government in a parliamentary system characterized by many parties and minority rule is characteristically narrower than in a two-party system, while the freedom of action in a two-party system is narrower than in a one-party system. As the range of options widens we approach oligarchy or dictatorship, as it narrows we approach anarchy and chaos. The social choices that emerge from the political process cannot be thought of as a single precise set of value judgements that constitute a welfare function, but rather as a range of possible courses of action that are potentially stable in the sense that they can survive. The greater the friction in the system, the higher the costs of overruling or changing an established government, the wider the range. If there were a single determinate best set of choices, then the narrower the range of possible policies open to government the closer would the outcome be to that optimum. When there is no such single optimum, however, the narrower the range open the greater the probability of instability, vacillation and intransitive circular sequences of reform, all effected at considerable cost.

The essence of the political problem is distribution, whether it be the distribution of income or of political power. A simple model[1] suffices to demonstrate the non-existence of a single determinate pattern of distribution and accordingly the non-existence of a single set of social choices. Figure 21 has already been explained in the context of the allocation of land to crops. We can think of it instead as representing a given total national income to be distributed among three persons, the relative shares being depicted by the lengths of the perpendiculars to the sides. Again there will be a two-to-one vote for movements into three zones and against movements into three others. If

1. For a more rigorous treatment of this theme see Plott (1967).

motives of altruism and envy exist the version encompassing indifference curves will be relevant with the same stringent conditions required for there to be an equilibrium. If, however, we assume that any person calling for a vote to change the existing distribution is required to pay a fee for the privilege, which will not be refunded if the outcome is reversed by a subsequent vote at the call of another party, then there may well be a range of points any one of which would be such that no vote to change it would be called. The higher the fee the wider would that range be. The fee introduces friction into the model and with friction there can be a stable outcome, albeit not a unique outcome. In the real world the friction derives from the cost and effort necessary to marshall sufficient political muscle to effect a change. Thus we see that the costs inherent in some ways of expressing relative strengths of individual preference, that were criticized on efficiency grounds in the previous section, may in the context of relating different individuals' preferences be the only way in which sufficient friction can be introduced into the system to achieve stability and avoid intransitive sequences of change. 'In a very real sense the workability of a democratic political system is contingent on its imperfections.' (Winch, 1969.)

A constitution is a distribution of political power, a set of rules for social decision making, but the one thing that a decision-making rule cannot be used to decide is what the decision-making rule should be. Provided that it is sufficiently acceptable not to be overthrown, a constitution will result in a government as a source of authority, and that government will be able to make and enforce value judgements concerning distribution and be able to exercise possibly wide powers of discretion. There is no basis in welfare economics for the contention that any constitution is better than another, nor that any concept of distributional equity is superior to another. Distributional value judgements emanate from government. Whatever they may be they constitute the basis of the welfare function that it is the task of policy to maximize. Welfare economics, however, does enable us to consider the alternative forms in which those value judgements might be expressed from the standpoint of logical consistency, and to deduce what policies concerning resource allocation are best calculated to maximize the government's welfare function. The subject is, however, limited to societies that encompass the Paretian value judgement within the emerging social values, for if that judgement is rejected the analysis of this book is irrelevant.

The form of the welfare function

In our discussion of the formal analysis of welfare maximization in a Paretian system, it was shown to be necessary that the welfare function be postulated in utility space. While necessary from the conceptual standpoint, the absence of any practicable index of utility makes it impossible to express or implement distributional value judgements in this form. Let us assume, however, that an optimum optimorum is achieved and examine its properties. Satisfaction of the exchange and production conditions would establish a set of price ratios for pure private goods and factors and for vectors of activities that encompass externalities (the relevant prices here making due allowances through taxes or subsidies for the local public bads or goods generated), together with certain volumes of pure public goods. Each individual would be just able to achieve a particular utility level, the set of such levels yielding the highest attainable level of welfare. The set of prices would constitute a constraint within which each individual could operate via exchange, given his initial endowment of factors and goods. While it is not in practice possible to stipulate the utility level that each individual should achieve it is possible to stipulate his endowment of factors and goods. Given the price ratios, any initial endowment that places him somewhere on the appropriate constraint would permit the individual to achieve his proper level of utility, and there is an infinity of such endowments for each individual. Thus in a perfect world, where a welfare optimum was achieved, it would be possible to express distributional value judgements in terms of volumes of factors or goods that would serve as proxy for an index of utility. While we could not stipulate the level of utility that he should be able to achieve, we could stipulate the constraint within which each individual should be permitted to operate. The essence of policy would be the stipulation of the relevant set of constraints.

While the real world is imperfect, policy does in fact manifest itself by stipulating constraints on individuals. Each is endowed with certain property rights and the ability to indulge in exchange through an imperfect set of markets. Price ratios are responsive to the actions of individuals in markets and may be influenced as a matter of policy by taxes or subsidies, or pegged by price controls. In addition all individuals are entitled to enjoy public goods, though these by their very nature cannot be exchanged. It is then conceptually possible to devise and implement policies that would achieve a welfare optimum, and it becomes possible for alternate policies to be assessed from the standpoint of welfare economics in terms of their appropriateness to the maximization of the apparent welfare function.

The initial endowment of factors and goods granted to a particular individual specifies only a point in factor–commodity space. The constraint through that point, which determines the level of utility he can achieve, is governed by the set of relative prices. While any point on the constraint is as good as any other for a given set of prices, two such points have quite different effects if relative prices change. In a dynamic world relative prices are subject to continual change through changes in both utility functions and production functions. Any initial chosen distribution expressed in terms of factors and goods, while appropriate initially, may become inappropriate either because the connection between endowment and utility changes through changes in relative prices, or because the distributional value judgements themselves change. In a dynamic world we must therefore expect the stipulation of distribution to be subject to continuous revision. Revisions can be accomplished in many ways. The pattern of factor ownership can be changed by death duties, capital levies, taxes on property, etc., with respect to land and capital, while the distribution of labour ownership can be changed by slavery, forced labour and conscription. Human capital can be redistributed through time by education policy. Goods can be redistributed by rationing or by their free provision as a public service. In a monetary system, transfers of income by taxes and subsidies can be used in place of transfers of factors and goods themselves. Finally, the effective price constraints can be manipulated by taxes, subsidies and controls to influence the relationship between initial endowment and achievable utility level. If this multitude of tools is used inconsistently or at random the cumulative effect through time can be extremely complicated and inefficient.

In general we can show that any change in distribution which is effected through quantitative changes in the endowments of factors is likely to be more efficient than one effected through changes in relative prices. In an exchange economy the achievement of a Paretian optimum calls for the determination of price ratios that equate marginal rates of substitution and transformation in the appropriate forms for both private and public goods. Any interference with those price ratios for distributional purposes will interfere with the efficient achievement of optimum allocation. The quantitative endowment that governs distribution is free from such restrictions. In practice, however, it is often simpler to manipulate price ratios than quantitative endowments.

The provision of public goods requires that resources be diverted from the production of private goods. The equity question of who should sacrifice is simply the question of the chosen distribution of the remaining private goods. It is quite distinct from the efficiency considerations of the alternate ways of achieving the resource transfer. The provision of public roads by statute labour accomplished the resource transfer by a change in the pattern of factor ownership. The factor labour belonged not to the individual but to the community for the specified number of hours. The inefficiency of this system arose through the suboptimal allocation of labour of different skills and abilities. When coupled with the right to commute statute labour by a money payment, however, this difficulty was in theory overcome. The system then became a poll tax that could be paid in either money or work. As such it was free from any distorting effects on price ratios.[1] Equally efficient was the use of taxes on the rental value of land.[2] Income taxes and excise taxes, however, do introduce distortions between the marginal productivity of labour and the marginal rates of substitution between goods and leisure. The distortion arises because the individual is left nominally owning factors and free to indulge in exchange, but is deterred from taking full advantage of exchange opportunities by the assessment of taxes on the sale of labour and the purchase of certain goods. When roads are congested they cease to be a pure public good and the use of excise taxes, e.g. on motor fuel, is then highly appropriate. Similar arguments apply to defence, the modern equivalent of statute labour being conscription. While the confiscation of the ownership and control of labour inherent in this form of slavery is free from price-ratio distortion, it suffers from all the allocational inefficiencies of statute labour, without the right to commute, and involves the unusual distributional value judgement that taxes should be paid for defence primarily by healthy young adult males. The theoretical advantages of transferring resources to the state by a direct redistribution of factor ownership, rather than by distorting marginal taxes on exchange, support the argument for land taxation and the public ownership of land and capital. We see this principle practised not only in socialist societies but in the reservation of mineral rights by the Crown.[3]

When the set of factor and product prices changes, the previously existing pattern of factor ownership may yield a quite different distribution of utility levels. When the change in relative market prices is temporary, as for example in the case of food shortages in wartime England, it can be offset as

1. This is not, of course, to assert that the system was in fact optimally administered, but rather that in theory it was a distortion-free form of taxation.

2. The use of taxes on rent was examined in our discussion of the marginal cost pricing principle.

3. Oil royalties have been a very important substitute for taxes in the province of Alberta, Canada, which is by no means a socialist society in other respects.

we have seen by the use of price controls and rationing. More permanent shifts cause greater difficulty and are the basic cause of the farm-income problem in North America. Rising productivity in agriculture, which produces goods for which there are both low price and income elasticities of demand, tends to reduce the utility levels of the owners of factors used in agriculture, while rising productivity in manufacturing, producing goods for which there is a high income elasticity of demand, may raise incomes for the owners of factors in that sector. The efficient solution, of course, is a transfer of resources from agriculture to manufacturing and the service industries, and income differentials have in fact resulted in a substantial shift of population from agriculture. In a private enterprise economy the initial inequitable effect on the distribution of utility is the very means by which efficient resource allocation is fostered. Any attempt to offset the inequity may hinder the efficient reallocation of resources. If it is desired to compensate those in agriculture for the costs incurred in moving, or for the permanent loss if jobs yielding incomes elsewhere that may be considered equitable are not available, various forms of compensation can be used. Direct grants that would not be contingent on remaining in agriculture would be the most efficient. Distortions of the price level by subsidies or price supports, while they may achieve the desired effect on relative utility levels, seriously jeopardize the efficient allocation of resources. The result is a surplus problem, and that may result in 'soil bank' schemes that make grants contingent on not using factors at all.

A comparable problem of growing concern in developed economies arises with widening market-price differentials for skilled and unskilled labour. The value judgement, that it would be desirable to reduce the inequality of income that resulted from inherited inequalities in the ownership of property, could be satisfied over time by death duties, even though these violated the traditional sanctity of private property. Where the inequality is in the ownership of human capital, however, the problem is more difficult. The gift of expensive education to those already blessed with native ability intensifies the inequality, even though it may encourage more optimal levels of production of human capital. To leave the ownership and control of human capital with the natural distribution, while offsetting the distributional consequences by manipulation of relative net wage levels, causes serious distortion in the price ratios that underlie the Paretian optimum. High marginal taxes on high-wage groups create a disincentive to work and an incentive to emigrate. The effect is either the wastage or loss of the human capital produced by subsidized education. Settlement of wage claims by lower income groups on the basis of equity rather than productivity may lead to high unemployment levels for which inflation is not a long-run cure. It also leads to an incentive for immigration by unskilled workers. Various forms of guaranteed income schemes are receiving extensive examination as possible solutions. Supplementing the incomes of those with low-valued endowments of factors must be distinguished from subsidy of those who choose not to use factors, however, to avoid disincentive effects. The appropriate means test is an income potential test, though this is easy neither to devise nor to administer. The transfer of income from those with high-valued factors is a still more difficult problem. Either one must divest the individual of sole ownership of human capital, a very unpopular proposal in light of the tradition of freedom of the person, or one can use high marginal tax rates with all their disincentive effects. The latter solution achieves equity at the expense of efficiency. Income potential rather than income as the tax base is again theoretically attractive but difficult to administer.

The socialist solution of directed labour, administered output plans and administered prices has severe shortcomings in a Paretian context. It is in practice virtually impossible to approximate Pareto optimality in such a system. The alternative of modified capitalism with extensive distortion of relative prices through marginal taxes and subsidies also falls far short of Pareto optimality, however. A second-best solution to the dilemma may well require recognition that the traditional use of property and labour rights, as proxy for utility *i because 'construct' before ~goals~ ~implicit~ no constant. (pp ℛ→)*

The Avowed Targets of Policy **195**

levels, as the medium through which distributional value
judgements are enforced, may not be sufficiently flexible to
accommodate adjustment to the rapidly changing technology
of the modern world. While welfare economics does not offer
a ready solution, it does enable us to analyse the problem and
identify the source of the difficulty.

The avowed targets of policy

The welfare economic theory of Pareto optimality, analysed
in the esoteric realms of utility space, appears far removed
from the real world issues of everyday economic policy.
There the goals are not maximization of a welfare function
in utility space but full employment, stable prices, a high rate
of growth, a viable balance of payments. These may well be
the appropriate means to welfare maximization, however.
Just as the distribution of factor ownership is an appropriate
medium through which to enforce distributional value
judgements concerning utility (provided that the true end is
kept in mind and sight is not lost of the changing relationship
between factor endowment and utility), so the shifting
outward of the constraints on individual choice, postulated in
factor-commodity space, is an appropriate way to increase
utility levels. The assumption of utility maximization by the
individual permits us to restate the Paretian value judgement.
The easing of constraints on the freedom of choice of one
individual, constraints of others being unaffected, leads to an
increase in welfare.

Pareto optimality is achieved through exchange. Anything
that facilitates the smooth and efficient functioning of an
exchange system tends to foster the achievement of Pareto
optimality. Money lubricates the machinery of barter and a
stable monetary system facilitates the achievement of optimality. Escalating inflation reduces confidence in money and
reduces its effectiveness as both a store of value and a medium
of exchange. Uneven inflation distorts relative real income
levels and price ratios, which may jeopardize the achievement
of both equity and efficiency. Clearly the fight to control
inflation is relevant to the maximization of welfare. But

inflation is not itself the evil, it is a potential impediment to achievement of the real objective. It does not follow that the optimal pace of inflation is zero. The hoarding of liquid balances deprives the machinery of exchange of its lubricant; the result may be a recession. This supports the contention that since inflation is a tax on liquidity and excessive liquidity preference may generate dynamic externalities in the nature of a public bad, the optimal pace of inflation may well be positive (see, for example, Winch, 1970). Others have argued on different grounds that the optimal pace of inflation is negative (see, for example, Friedman, 1969). Clearly there is agreement that inflation is relevant to welfare, but welfare economics is currently too little developed in the field of macrodynamics for its relevance to be fully understood. Optimality may require a policy on inflation, but what that policy should be is another matter. The danger is that control of forces that influence the achievement of welfare may be treated as ends in themselves, with little or no thought to examination of the intricate relationships that exist between those forces and the achievable level of welfare. The contention that we should fight any inflation is not self-evident; it invites the serious question, why? No fully satisfactory answer to that question is currently available.

In an open economy, exchange is an international business. Just as fluctuations in the internal value of money may hinder the achievement of maximum welfare through exchange, so fluctuations in the relationships between currencies mitigate against optimal patterns of exchange internationally. This is the case for stable exchange rates. The exchange rate between two currencies, however, governs (together with internal price levels) the effective price ratio between traded goods. Optimal exchange requires appropriate international as well as internal price ratios if Pareto optimality is to be achieved. If stabilization of the wrong exchange rates is pushed to the length of maintaining distorted price ratios between imports and exports, one impediment to welfare maximization is generated in the cause of controlling another. Distorted exchange rates can influence international distribution, and determination of an optimum exchange rate policy, together with optimum tariff policy, requires international distributional value judgements. An optimal policy for the maximization of internal welfare may be quite different from that appropriate for the maximization of world welfare if utility of foreigners is judged to be as important as utility of one's own citizens. Short-term expedients to mitigate fluctuations in exchange rates or exchange reserves often focus on the influence on short-term capital movements that can be achieved by manipulation of interest rates. But interest rates also influence investment, and unstable interest rates mitigate against welfare maximization through time, just as an unstable pace of inflation and unstable exchange rates hinder welfare maximization through current exchange.

The optimal social rate of time preference was considered in our discussion of cost–benefit analysis. It concerns the optimal level of investment, which in turn governs the optimal rate of growth. It was there argued that the optimum rate of interest may involve social considerations that transcend expressions of private time preference. The optimum rate of growth is an appropriate goal of economic policy, but what the appropriate growth rate is will depend on the welfare function. Just as an optimum tariff policy rests on distributional value judgements between ourselves and foreigners, so an optimal growth policy rests on similar judgements between ourselves and our descendants. The optimal rate of growth is certainly not the maximum achievable unless zero weight is attached to the utility of the present generation.

The secret of success in the market is to sell dear and buy cheap. The most favourable constraint through any initial endowment is one that reflects the highest prices for the things one sells and the lowest for the things one buys. Therein lies the popular appeal of the political promise of high wages and cheap goods. If wage rates are permitted to rise above value productivity, however, the result can only be rising prices (i.e. inflation), subsidy (i.e. distorting marginal taxes), or a reduction in the quantities exchanged (i.e. unemployment). If the last outcome is rejected, as it is where full employment is a goal of policy, then one must be prepared for either subsidized employment or continuous and possibly accelerating inflation unless by some means wage rates are prevented from rising above value productivity. If equity considerations concerning what income an individual should receive enter as criteria in determining wage rates, then subsidy or inflation are the likely outcomes. The situation is then analytically the same as the farm poverty problem. To assist farmers by maintaining artificially high prices for their products involves either subsidy or surplus. To assist employees by permitting negotiated wage rates to rise above productivity has the same consequence. The surplus in this case is, of course, surplus labour or unemployment. Both are examples of the consequences of using the price system not simply for the task of resource allocation, which is its central role in a market economy, but also as a means for achieving distributional objectives. Clearly, full employment, stable prices and efficient resource allocation are compatible only if factor prices (including wages) are used to govern resource allocation while other means are employed to achieve distributional equity.

That efficiency of the economic system is a proper goal of policy is a truism. Whatever the chosen distribution, Paretian improvements are possible unless a Paretian optimum is achieved. Efficiency in the allocation of resources calls not only for a public sector that will provide for the production of public goods, but for policies to mitigate the inadequacies of an imperfect market structure. Externalities have been discussed in the context of public goods and bads; allowance for them may call for regulation, taxes or subsidies. Imperfect competition may lead to divergencies from optimal price ratios and the more extreme cases of monopoly may call for control. The entire market system may be subject to dynamic fluctuations that result in intermittent failure to utilize resources efficiently, or even to utilize them at all. Full employment in this respect is an appropriate goal of stabilization policy, but full employment at efficient wage-to-price ratios is a goal quite distinct from full employment at distorted wage-to-price ratios that are sanctioned for distributional motives.

Conclusions

Any policy can be discussed rationally only in the context of the appropriate means to the achievement of some objective. The edifice of welfare economics is built on the premise that a more or less clearly defined objective is formulated by government through the political process. Complex economic theory is involved in analysing the relationships between the esoteric realm of utility space in which the objective exists conceptually and the everyday issues of economic policy. In the context of comparative statics the theory is well developed. Little progress has, however, been made in welfare dynamics and the dynamic world is clearly a second-best one. The inability of welfare economists to devise and agree on rigorously formulated solutions to the pressing problems of policy should not, however, blind us to the fact that all problems of economic policy are problems of economic welfare. If attention is focused only on achieving means, while the shifting relationships between means and ends are overlooked, the diverse tools of economic policy may be misused. The commonly evoked targets of full employment, stable prices, etc. are not goals, they are means. To think of choosing among alternate mixes of incompatible means by value judgement is nonsense. Value judgements are the basis of objectives; the choice of appropriate means to achieve a given end is the task of analysis. Much work remains to be done before economists can take pride in their ability to perform that task. Meanwhile governments muddle through. But to complacently believe that the formulation of policy is directly and simply a matter of value judgements, and accordingly neither the business nor the responsibility of the discipline of economics, is to deny that we live in a Paretian world.

The Paretian value judgement is only a value judgement. It may well be rejected by some. But before it is rejected by economists, either explicitly or by implication, it must be remembered that virtually the entire edifice of economic theory as we know it today is built on Paretian premises. If those premises are rejected, that theory becomes irrelevant to the world in which we live. Faced with the policy issues of the modern world, economics in its present state is either inadequate or irrelevant, and economists are the practitioners of that art. The more this is realized and the greater the effort to remedy the situation, the sooner will it be possible to label this book obsolete.

References

Arrow, K. J. (1963), *Social Choice and Individual Values*, Wiley, 2nd edn.

Breton, A. (1966), 'A theory of the demand for public goods', *Canad. J. Econ. and polit. Sci.*, November, pp. 455–67.

Clawson, M. (1959), 'Methods of measuring the demand for and value of outdoor recreation', *Resources for Future Inc.*, Washington D.C.

Coleman, J. S. (1966), 'The possibility of a social welfare function', *Amer. econ. Rev.*, December, pp. 1105–22.

Dickinson, H. D. (1933), 'Price formation in a socialist community', *Econ. J.*, vol. XLIII, pp. 237–50.

Friedman, M. (1969), *The Optimum Quantity of Money*, Aldine, Chicago.

Henderson, P. D. (1968), 'Investment criteria for public enterprises', in *Public Enterprise* (ed. R. Turvey), Penguin.

Hicks, J. R. (1956), *A Revision of Demand Theory*, Oxford University Press.

Hotelling, H. (1938), 'The general welfare in relation to problems of taxation and of railway and utility rates', *Econometrica*, vol. VI, pp. 242–69.

Lipsey, R. G., and Lancaster K., (1956–7), 'The general theory of second best', *Rev. econ. Stud.*, vol. 24, pp. 11–32.

Little, I. M. D. (1957), *A Critique of Welfare Economics*, Oxford University Press.

McManus, M. (1959), 'Comments on the general theory of second best', *Rev. econ. Stud.*, vol. 26, pp. 209–24.

Marglin, S. A. (1963), 'The social rate of discount and the optimal rate of investment', *Q. J. Econ.*, February, pp. 95–111.

Mishan, E. J. (1962), 'Second thoughts on the second best', *Oxford econ. Papers*, October, pp. 205–77.

Mishan, E. J. (1964), *Welfare Economics*, Random House.

Plott, C. R. (1967), 'Equilibrium and majority rule', *Amer. econ. Rev.*, September, pp. 787–806.

Prest, A. R., and Turvey, R. (1965), 'Cost-benefit analysis: a survey', *Econ. J.*, December, pp. 683–735.

Ruggles, N. (1949–50a), 'The welfare basis of the marginal cost pricing principle', *Rev. econ. Stud.*, vol. 17, pp. 29–46.

RUGGLES, N. (1949–50b), 'Recent developments in the theory of marginal cost pricing', *Rev. econ. Stud.*, vol. 17, pp. 107–26.

SAVOSNICK, K. M. (1958), 'The box diagram and the production possibility curve', *Ekonomisk Tidscrift*, vol. 60, September, pp. 183–97.

SCITOVSKY, T. (1941), 'A note on welfare propositions in economics', *Rev. econ. Stud.*, vol. 9, November, pp. 77–88.

TRICE, A. H., and WOOD, S. E. (1958), 'Measurement of recreation benefits', *Land Econ.*, vol. XXXIV, August, pp. 195–207.

WINCH, D. M. (1963), *The Economics of Highway Planning*, University of Toronto Press.

WINCH, D. M. (1965), 'Consumer's surplus and the compensation principle', *Amer. econ. Rev.*, June, pp. 395–423.

WINCH, D. M. (1969), 'Pareto, public goods and politics', *Canad. J. Econ.*, November, pp. 492–508.

WINCH, D. M. (1970), 'Inflation and resource allocation', *McMaster University, Department of Economics Working Paper*, no. 70–11.

WORLAND, S. T. (1967), *Scholasticism and Welfare Economics*, University of Notre Dame Press.

Index